Heartful Spanish

Your Joyful Path to Fluency

LOUISA BURFORD

*This workbook is dedicated with love to my mum
and the memory of my dad.
Thank you for sharing with us your love of travel
and your openness and curiosity to learn languages.*

"Life is really simple, but we insist on making it complicated."

"La vida es muy sencilla, pero insistimos en hacerla complicada."

~ Confucius, Chinese philosopher, fifth century BC

"Language learning is really simple,
but we insist on making it complicated."

*"El aprendizaje de idiomas es muy sencillo,
pero insistimos en hacerlo complicado."*

~ Me (borrowing from Confucius a little)

Disclaimer:

The guidance and strategies found in this book may not be suitable for every situation. This work is sold with the understanding that the author is not held responsible for the results that ensue as a direct or indirect consequence of following the advice in this book.

Author's note:

I have no affiliation with the websites, applications, online communities, or other resources recommended in this workbook. If something has worked for me or I've tried it and it looks promising, I recommend it. Just spreading the love!

Copyright © 2023 Louisa Burford

All rights reserved.

No part of this publication may be reproduced, distributed, or transmitted in any form or by any means, including photocopying, recording, or other electronic or mechanical methods, without the prior written permission of the copyright owner, except in the case of brief quotations for book reviews and certain other non-commercial uses permitted by copyright law.

Title: Heartful Spanish: your joyful path to fluency
Name: Burford, Louisa, author
Book design by Jonas Perez Studio
Proofreading by Sydney Owens

TABLE OF CONTENTS

INTRODUCTION   13
    A bit of background   15
    A bit about me   17
    Why traditional teaching methods don't always work   20
    What is fluency anyway?   21
    How to use this workbook   22
    Why learn Spanish and how can we make the process fun and easy?   24
    A Lamborghini in your garage   25

YOUR VISION   27
    Why your vision is important   29
    Set an intention for your Spanish learning   29
    Visualise your "big picture" Spanish goal   32
    Creative visualisation for your Spanish goal   34
    Learning like a baby learns: open and curious   35

THE HEART AND THE EMOTIONS   39
    Heart or mind?   41
    Mindfulness, the emotions, and language learning   42
    Heart energy   44

AFFIRMATION POWER   47
    How affirmations work   49
    Affirmations to supercharge your Spanish   50
    Write down your feel-good affirmations   53
    Personal prayer or affirmation of openness to possibility   54

GRATITUDE — 59
  A word on the power of gratitude — 61
  Advance gratitude — 61

BUSTING THROUGH YOUR BLOCKS — 65
  A word about blocks — 67
  Busting through Block #1: "I don't have time to learn Spanish." — 69
  Busting through Block #2: "I don't want to spend money on learning Spanish." — 84
  Busting through Block #3: "The vocab never seems to stick." — 87
  Busting through Block #4: "I never get the opportunity to talk with native speakers." — 90
  Busting through Block #5: "I'm embarrassed to make mistakes." — 94
  Busting through Block #6: "I'm embarrassed about my accent." — 97
  Busting through Block #7: "I can't get motivated to practise/study Spanish." — 101
  Busting through Block #8: "I can't understand Spanish speakers. It all goes over my head!" — 109
  Busting through Block #9: "I can't do this!" or "I'm no good at languages!" — 115

BRINGING IN THE JOY FACTOR — 129
  Joyful activities brainstorming — 131
  Brainstorm new ways to combine your joyful activities with learning Spanish — 133
  A word on finding joy in immersion — 137
  Your energy and your "vibes" — 138
  Notice your vibes around learning Spanish — 140

YOUR NEW FEEL-GOOD LEARNING STRATEGY — 143
  What is a feel-good language learning strategy? — 145
  Brainstorm ideas for your new feel-good learning plan — 147
  Your new feel-good Spanish learning plan — 148
  A note on keeping it "feel-good" — 150

BUILDING CONSISTENCY — 151
  Track your progress — 153
  Find an accountability buddy or group — 154
  Notice how far you've come — 154

SOME SOS TOOLS AND TIPS — 157
  Self-compassion and acceptance — 159

Affirmations for a reset	160
Set a new tiny goal and commit to it	161
If you've burnt out, take a break	161
EFT tapping	161

RESOURCES: MINDSET, JOY, & SUCCESS — **167**

Books	169
Podcasts	176
YouTube	177
Websites	178
Apps	180
Courses	181
Communities	182
Articles and academic works consulted	183

RESOURCES FOR YOUR SPANISH — **187**

Instagram	189
Learn Spanish on YouTube	192
Other YouTube channels in Spanish	193
Spanish radio	198
Podcasts for Spanish learners	199
Podcasts in Spanish on other subjects	201
Other useful websites for your Spanish	203
Apps for your Spanish	207
Books	208
TV series in Spanish	215
Chrome extensions for subtitles	216
Spanish and Latin American cinema	217

SHINE YOUR LIGHT — **221**

Go forth on your own unique journey	223
Next steps	225
Let's connect	225
Spread the word	225

ACKNOWLEDGEMENTS — **227**

INTRODUCTION

"Every new beginning comes from some other beginning's end."
"Cada nuevo comienzo viene del final de algún otro comienzo."
~ Seneca, Stoic philosopher, 4th century BC

· *Introduction* ·

A BIT OF BACKGROUND

"The mind is not a vessel to be filled but a fire to be ignited." This gorgeous sentence, uttered by Plutarch nearly 2,000 years ago, sums up exactly my philosophy on language learning. You can learn all the words in the dictionary, but if you don't have fun, practising Spanish in a way that feels good to you and ignites your curiosity and enjoyment of the language, you're unlikely to get to the feeling of ease and flow that is fluency. First, we focus on the positive emotion, and then we feel the flow.

Despite what you may have experienced to the contrary, languages are not difficult. Everyone who has learnt their own native language to fluency can learn another language with ease. All that is needed is a combination of the right circumstances and mindset. *And the key is to have fun!*

Traditional teaching methods tend to be a lot less effective than simply diving in and learning the language by trial and error, listening to joy-spreading individuals talk about what they're passionate about, and chatting to real people about subjects that interest you. If that sounds scary to you right now, it's OK, my love. I'll take you through some ways to get there in tiny steps. *Poco a poco.* [Little by little.]

As part of my Postgraduate Diploma in Teaching Spanish as a Foreign Language 17 years ago, I learnt about how the neglect of Romanian infants in orphanages in the 1980s seriously affected their language acquisition. The lack of human contact and attention meant the children suffered from serious deficits in cognitive function and language development compared with non-institutionalised children and others who were placed in foster homes (Nelson et al., 2014). This tragic example points to the importance of human interaction and engagement with the senses and the emotions in language acquisition, a perspective that underlies an increasingly popular language teaching method known as "content-based" language instruction (Snow & Brinton, 2017).

In content-based language teaching, teachers introduce interesting topics to talk about in the foreign language, so the students engage with the subject matter itself, picking up the language almost as an afterthought. This is much closer to the way we naturally learn languages than other teaching methods, and it resonated with me deeply when I learnt about it.

You see, despite my lifelong dedication to and love of learning languages, mostly in formal educational settings, I would estimate that *95% of my fluency came from immersion in real life*. I've lived in six different countries and soaked up the language like a sponge with heaps of fun and enjoyment each time. My experience has shown me that this is by far the fastest way to learn languages, and it is relatively effortless in comparison with more theoretical methods.

The combination of learning by immersion and content-based learning is the raison d´être of my heart-centred language learning project, The Heartful Spanish Podcast. It's a bilingual podcast (and accompanying Instagram account) about all things personal growth, spirituality, and language learning, three subjects I'm passionate about. The idea is that the topics discussed will hopefully resonate with language learners who have similar interests to me, and they will soak up the language effortlessly.

It has never been easier to immerse yourself in a foreign language in tiny doses, because today's magical tech enables you to do it at the touch of a screen, whenever and wherever you like. The possibilities this brings are endless, and frankly, I'm in total awe.

The aim of this workbook is to teach you an innovative approach to learning Spanish. Imagine what you could do if you believed in yourself and your language abilities more. I hope to inspire you to have a lot more fun while you're at it too.

· *Introduction* ·

No matter how your Spanish journey has been so far, it's time to look at it with fresh eyes. All that's needed is that you're open to trying new things.

A BIT ABOUT ME

In case we've not met, here's a bit about me and why I've created this workbook. I'm Louisa, a translator specialising in the field of psychology, and I'm passionate about personal growth, spirituality, and languages. Although I've learnt five languages to fluency (including my native English), I've had a bit of an inferiority complex most of my life about "just speaking languages", firstly because everyone can do it (more on that later) and secondly because I don't have a "useful" specialism like my more scientific and logical friends and family members.

Luckily, a life of soul-searching has led me—via a million self-help books, personal growth courses, and much dabbling in different fields—to find my calling. I feel this is what I'm meant to be doing: applying my accumulated tips and tricks to create a deeply intuitive, joy-based, self-led, heart-centred approach to language learning for people who need a little help finding ease and joy in their Spanish journey. I'm excited to share this innovative approach with you.

The Spanish language has always held a special kind of magic for me. My first recollections of learning the language go back to when I was about seven or eight years old, skipping along a dusty road in Majorca one summer, my little hand clinging onto my dad's strong, solid palm while he taught me to count to ten. *Uno... dos... tres... cuatro... cinco... seis... siete... ocho... nueve... diez.* A mysterious new code to decipher. What a delight!

Some years later, when I was 13, the long-awaited moment came for me to start learning Spanish at school. I had high hopes for—

and wonderful associations with—the language; some of our best family holidays were in Spain when I was growing up, especially in the beautiful Balearic Islands.

However, I can clearly remember a moment, just a few short months into my Spanish education, when my initial excitement disappeared down the drain in a flash. Sitting in a Spanish lesson one dreary winter afternoon, in Room 34 with the lights too bright and the heating too high, 13-year-old me got my first taste of verb tables. *¡Madre mía!* [Literally: Mother mine!] Until then, we'd mostly just spent the classes memorising quite useless and boring phrases (which I even rather enjoyed, still riding the wave of positive associations from our Majorca holidays). But this was a whole new level of hell—and uselessness.

I'd never felt so confused and lost in my life. I remember feeling utterly panicked in that suffocating classroom. My Spanish joy bubble burst right there and then. *Mi gozo en un pozo* [literally: "My delight in a well", meaning "My illusion was shattered"]. How could there just be one word to say, for example, "I have"? (*Tengo*). Where was the subject? Like "*Je suis*" in French or "I am" in English. Aargh! I found the whole thing excruciatingly incomprehensible, meaningless, and a little bit terrifying.

I managed to muddle on through the next classes, and I eventually got the hang of verb tables whilst not quite seeing the point of them (and I still stand by that opinion now, a few Hispanic Studies degrees and diplomas later).

Luckily, not long after that fateful encounter with Spanish verb tables, I had a massive language-learning epiphany when I spent two weeks at the home of a wonderful French family in Lyon. Now, I wouldn't have said I was fluent in French at that time or anything like that, but post-Lyon, everything suddenly clicked into place with my French. After just two weeks of immersion in the language, sharing a room with a French girl of my age and living and breathing *français* the entire time, I now had the wonderful certainty that I could find a way to say pretty much anything I needed to, and I could understand most things too. *I had found my flow in French.*

The following year, when I was 14, I spent three weeks at the home of a Spanish family in Barcelona on a school exchange and had a similar experience, but the transformation was even more dramatic. Spanish is a much easier language to learn than French, and my knowledge of French hugely boosted my ability to understand and speak Spanish. Plus, I had all those positive associations of Spain from family holidays in sunny places, and—most importantly—*I now knew that it was possible to learn languages easily by immersion, with little effort and lots of fun.*

After my school exchanges (which I did a couple more of in subsequent years), I got A's in Spanish and French pretty much all through school, despite dedicating very little time and effort to memorising verb tables or vocab lists. I'm so deeply grateful my parents made it a priority for my brothers and me to do exchanges when we were teenagers. What a fabulous language hack! Effortless A's! Why didn't everyone do this, I wondered.

You see, the fastest way to learn a language is to soak it up by immersion, like a baby learns—eyes and ears open, with curiosity and interest. The more we engage our senses and emotions, the easier and more natural the language acquisition becomes. All of us learnt our native language effortlessly, and we can do it again with a second (third, fourth, etc.) language in a similar way.

WHY TRADITIONAL TEACHING METHODS DON'T ALWAYS WORK

I've seen too many of my friends and family members get blocked with traditional methods of learning Spanish. Boring classes and uninspiring language materials can lead to a lack of motivation to learn and an "I can't" mentality. We learn best when we are uplifted and inspired, and when we are interested and engaged in the content and having fun while we practise, *so it doesn't feel like hard work.*

Language learning doesn't happen in a vacuum. It happens best by soaking up the sights, sounds, and smells of a culture with lots of emotion and human connection. Fluency comes from lived experiences; rarely does it happen in the classroom alone.

This is why many people struggle with traditional language classes or even language apps; they can often be dull and rigid, and lacking the one thing that will help you get fluent fast—*full engagement with all the senses and the emotions whilst having fun.* For those who have a natural interest in languages and want to gain a qualification, traditional-style classes or newer language apps can provide a structure and measurements to guide and assess your learning process. But by far the fastest, most fun way to reach fluency is through immersion, by going to the country and engaging with all your senses and emotions and communicating with native speakers.

If that last paragraph made your heart sink because that hasn't been your experience of immersion at all—perhaps you've even moved to Spain or Latin America and you're finding it anything but quick and easy to pick up the lingo—fear not, my dear, I have exercises to help you undo the mental blocks that are holding you back. I know all the obstacles to fluency because I've been there too at different phases in my experience of learning languages. Thankfully, in this amazing internet age, we can replicate the immersion experience in a doable way through what I call "mini-immersions": consuming real Spanish, preferably spoken (and written) by native speakers, in small doses every day.

> **Top tip**
>
> If you're currently at the stage where the mere thought of sitting down to dedicate time to your Spanish fills you with dread or negativity, try coupling this workbook with something that feels like a treat to you—take it to the park and sit under a tree, play some upbeat music (either before you open this book or as you work through it), or take it somewhere nice, like a café, beach, or somewhere in nature. You could turn it into a ritual by lighting a candle or some incense to signify that this is a new, conscious, heart-centred way of tending to your Spanish fluency dream.

WHAT IS FLUENCY ANYWAY?

Fluency is an incredibly subjective experience. The only person who can decide if you're fluent in a language is you. And yet, paradoxically, if you go around saying "I'm fluent", you sound like a bit of a nob!

The origin of the word "fluency" comes from the Latin word *fluere* meaning "to flow". Fluency is exactly that—a feeling of flow and ease when speaking (listening to, writing, etc.) a language. And like all feelings, it comes and goes. Some days you might feel more fluent than others. That's completely normal.

In my blog, My Little Spanish Notebook, I call it "the F word". It's an absurd word really, and one that we place far too much importance on, as if reaching fluency gained you a badge of honour that you could display on your puffed-out chest forever more, never again to make a mistake, be lost for words, or misunderstand anything in that language.

Ha! That's where we're going wrong, my friend. We often think of fluency as some kind of far-off tropical island paradise—difficult to reach, always on the horizon, and not even in sight when the waves are choppy. We confuse being fluent with being perfect. And being perfect is a ridiculous goal, in life and in languages, as I hope you'll agree.

We are already perfect, each in our own way. Perfectly imperfect, actually. And we have to love ourselves through the difficult spots and cultivate self-compassion and positive self-talk to help ourselves find ease and flow more easily, in language learning and in life itself. The "insular Tahiti" is within us all the time. Finding ease and flow is an inside job.

And that's exactly what we'll be tackling in this workbook. I'll help you create a process and mindset to help you get your Spanish to flow more easily. And please promise me that, from now on, whenever you hear or read the word "fluent" or "fluency", you'll remember that it just means "flow", which is something readily available to us all at any time and not some far-off, impossible "someday" goal.

HOW TO USE THIS WORKBOOK

This workbook is designed to be a self-led resource for you to work through at your own pace. I recommend you work through the whole book as best you can. Feel free to skip any exercises that don't feel right to you though. Once you've finished the workbook, you can use it as an SOS and dip back into it as and when you need a boost to your joyful Spanish practice.

The Your Vision section is arguably the most important one. You will come back to this section often, so it will be useful to

· *Introduction* ·

either bookmark the pages if you're writing in the book or copy them out on a loose sheet of paper for easy reference. Most of the other brainstorming exercises can be done just fine in any journal or notebook you have at home. (Fellow stationery lovers, I encourage you to treat yourself to a gorgeous new notebook to mark the start of your new joyful journey to fluency.)

After your first work-through, any time you feel yourself losing your Spanish mojo, just pick the workbook back up and do an exercise or two to bring you back to feeling motivated again. Simply follow your intuition and choose the activities that appeal the most to you, always with an attitude of openness and curiosity. You'll be back on your feet again in no time.

In language learning—like in life itself—you get out what you put in. And it's the same with this workbook: the more exercises you do, the more often you do them, and the more you engage with the activities, the bigger the shift you will experience in your Spanish. If you do the exercises with enthusiasm and an open mind, you will soon start to see a huge improvement.

Over the following pages, I will guide you through the process of creating a new path ahead for you, one that leaves you feeling confident in yourself and your ability to speak Spanish, so you stop seeing your language practice as yet another obligation to keep putting off, and instead, you actually enjoy it and *want* to commit to doing it more.

This approach is nothing like anything you've done before. It will empower you to develop the mindset and habits you need to take you from where you are now to where you want to be on your fluency journey. It will show you how to keep your Spanish practice feeling good, which will help you stay consistent and keep showing up with joy in your heart—the key to making fast, effortless progress.

Come back to this workbook whenever you're feeling in need of a boost to your Spanish joy levels.

I'm so excited for you. You can turn it all around in an instant. You'll see.

WHY LEARN SPANISH AND HOW CAN WE MAKE THE PROCESS FUN AND EASY?

The difference between travelling (or living) in a country where you speak the language proficiently and one where you don't is huge. Speaking Spanish opens up a whole world of possibilities—job or business opportunities, travel, friendships, fun, self-confidence, you name it. I can't wait for you to see for yourself where it will take you.

Spanish is a beautiful language, and it's easy to learn. How quickly you become fluent in Spanish will depend on how much time, effort, and—most importantly—*fun* you put into your learning. Experts generally agree that it's much easier and quicker to reach fluency in Spanish than it is in most other languages.

You start by listening out for what are known in the linguistic world as "cognates"—words that have the same origin, allowing you to understand them with little or no effort. You'll be surprised at how many there are in Spanish. Here are some examples of cognates in Spanish for English speakers: *procrastinación* (procrastination), *problema* (problem), *bagaje* (baggage/luggage), and *fantástico* (fantastic).

For English speakers (and those who already speak other Romance languages like French or Italian), the large number of cognates in Spanish, coupled with the fact that it's a very phonetic language—i.e., it's written pretty much exactly as it sounds, once you've learnt a few basic pronunciation rules—means that just by listening to Spanish, you can pick up a lot and learn quickly.

· *Introduction* ·

A LAMBORGHINI IN YOUR GARAGE

I want you to know that your Spanish fluency awaits you, like a beautiful Lamborghini that you didn't even know you had in your garage. You've had the ignition keys in your hand all along. Now it's time to open your eyes, really *see* that beauty, and make a decision on how you're going to drive it. If your default Spanish mode is self-criticism, effort, and struggle, it will be like driving your luxury sports car with the handbrake on or never getting out of first gear. If instead you intentionally choose joy, ease, and fun for your Spanish journey, it'll be a case of accelerator pedal to the floor and top gear cruising all the way.

I'm here to help you come up with new ways to find joy and ease in your Spanish journey. Before you know it, you'll be cruising along in that fabulous Lamborghini you had in the garage all the time.

Fun fact:

Did you know, Lamborghinis are named after real life Spanish "hero" bulls? Ones that gave the *matador* a run for their money. Just for the record, bullfighting repulses me. I could never watch a "sport" like that. But until it is banned, I will always be on the side of the bull.

YOUR VISION

"It's delightful when your imaginations come true, isn't it?"

"Es maravilloso cuando lo que has imaginado se hace realidad, ¿a que sí?"

~ L. M. Montgomery, author of Anne of Green Gables

WHY YOUR VISION IS IMPORTANT

In the field of psychology, there's growing evidence for an innovative treatment called "episodic future thinking", whereby patients repeatedly imagine themselves at future moments in their lives doing things that involve healthier choices and contribute to their long-term goals, enabling them to learn to make better decisions and overcome their negative patterns and addictive behaviours (see Aonso-Diego et al., 2023; Daniel et al., 2013).

If you imagine your desired outcome repeatedly and with enough emotion and detail, it will start to create a new mental blueprint of what's possible for you, and your subconscious mind will guide your decisions and actions in the direction of your goal until it becomes a reality in your life.

This is why we dedicate a whole section to helping you get clear on your vision for your Spanish fluency dream. We will refer back to this section often throughout the workbook to reinforce your clarity on your goals and boost your motivation to help you keep going in the right direction. The stronger the vision, the easier the path.

SET AN INTENTION FOR YOUR SPANISH LEARNING

First things first, let's set an intention for your language learning. What do you want to achieve from setting out on this journey? Are you aiming for fluency and the confidence to be able to express yourself in all or most situations? Or are you just looking to communicate better in a few specific situations—on holiday, when sightseeing, in your life as an expat in Spain or Latin America, at your kids' school, or with clients or colleagues, perhaps? Maybe you want to increase your vocabulary and improve your ability to conjugate verbs correctly. Or perhaps a feel-good goal for you would simply be to remember more of the new words you learn.

Take a moment to get quiet, listen to your inner wisdom, and jot down your intentions below and on the next page.

· *Your Vision* ·

More space for you to get clear on your intentions for your Spanish learning...

VISUALISE YOUR "BIG PICTURE" SPANISH GOAL

How do you want to *feel* when you're speaking Spanish? What experiences and emotions would you like to have? What will be possible for you when you've reached your goal? Who do you want to *become*? And how would this make you feel?

I encourage you to really push the boat out and go for big, seemingly impossible dreams. We're aiming for a huge breakthrough here, a massive achievement, new opportunities, wonderful connections, cherished friendships, heartfelt communication, or even a new identity.

Write freely on anything that comes up for you, *especially the feelings and emotions you want to experience when you've reached your goal.*

· *Your Vision* ·

Here's a little more space to explore the new possibilities your fluency goal will bring and the new identity you will embody when you've reached your big picture goal.

CREATIVE VISUALISATION FOR YOUR SPANISH GOAL

In her book, *Creative Visualization*, Shakti Gawain brings together Eastern philosophies and Western psychology to provide a series of simple exercises that will help you create the life of your dreams. When I first read it about 12 years ago, I immediately started practising creative visualisation regularly, and heaps of hitherto "impossible" dreams started appearing magically in my life.

In case you're interested, here are a few of the things I manifested that completely blew my mind: a lovely young American nanny who offered to look after my kids for less than half the going hourly rate; full-time paid writing work; and my dream house that ticked all the boxes, including views of the mountains and "lots of places to do meditation and yoga". Twelve years later, I'm still discovering new yoga and meditation spots in my house!

If you're open to giving it a try and applying it to your Spanish, check out some of the creative visualisation exercises either in Shakti Gawain's book or on YouTube, and have some fun imagining the things you've brainstormed in the previous exercise.

I'll leave you with my favourite exercise from Shakti Gawain's book, the pink bubble technique, adapted to help you focus on boosting your Spanish.

THE PINK BUBBLE TECHNIQUE

Follow these steps for the Heartful Spanish version of the pink bubble technique.

1. Take a few deep breaths to relax your body.
2. Feel your body sink into the chair or the surface you are resting on.
3. Progressively relax all the main muscle groups around your

body, starting at the top of your head and working down to the soles of your feet.

4. Now imagine the situations—and especially the feelings—you've described in your visualisation brainstorming above, *as if they were already your reality*. Add as much detail as possible about how you will feel when you reach your Spanish goals. Take your time. Most importantly, make sure you have fun with it.

5. Place your dream Spanish scenarios and all the wonderful feelings you've envisaged into a gorgeous big pink bubble in front of you.

6. When you're satisfied you've imagined your ideal outcome in enough detail, let the bubble go. Watch as your beautiful pink bubble lifts off into the air, taking with it your dream scenarios, accomplishments, and feelings off up to the atmosphere and away. You don't need to give it any more thought. Just trust that it is on its way.

7. Say, "This, or something better, is on its way to me now. Thank you, thank you, thank you."

LEARNING LIKE A BABY LEARNS: OPEN AND CURIOUS

At the beginning of this workbook, I said that the fastest way to become fluent in a language is to learn by immersion, engaging all the senses and emotions, similar to how we learnt to speak our native language as a baby. This assertion is the guiding principle of my heart-centred language learning approach.

Babies are born perfectly accepting of themselves exactly as they are. They contemplate the world around them with the utmost wonder and curiosity, and they follow their instinctive pull towards the things that bring them joy. They try new things, they mimic what they see and hear, and they don't yet have the conditioning or mindset issues that life experience tends to cloud us older humans with.

Every harsh word or ridicule from an adult or peer can undo that initial self-accepting, curious mindset and create emotional blockages that lead to fear and anxiety. We learn to second-guess ourselves. We see ourselves through the eyes of others. We worry we are not enough.

It's time to let all that go, my love. It's no longer serving us—in life or in language learning. Begin to see yourself soaking up the Spanish language effortlessly, the way you learnt your native tongue as a baby. Know that you can do this. Keep coming back to this "beginner's mind" any time your Spanish journey feels like an uphill struggle. Simply remember: babies do it best. Choose curiosity and playfulness, and watch the ease and fun flow in.

"BABY YOU" PROGRESSIVE RELAXATION AND VISUALISATION EXERCISE

Here is a relaxation and visualisation exercise to help you access your wise inner self, who already knows how to learn languages the joyful, curious way because you did it when you were a baby.

Content warning: This exercise involves visualising yourself as a baby. If you have any reason to think this could potentially be triggering for you, feel free to skip it or alternatively consult your therapist before you give it a try.

Relax. Take a few slow, deep breaths.

Gradually relax every muscle in your body.

Feel your body sink into the surface you are resting on.

Count from one to ten, slowly. With each number, feel your body becoming heavier and more relaxed.

Now visualise yourself as a baby, perhaps eight months old or so.

Lying on your back, kicking your feet in the air delightedly.

· Your Vision ·

Or perhaps sitting in your highchair, playing with a spoon.

The adults in your life talk to you with love in their voices.

You don't understand every word they're saying, but you are intrigued.

You piece bits together, and you get the gist.

You know when they are being adoring.

You know when they are angry or fearful.

You know when food is coming.

Or when someone wants to play with you.

You watch their every move with interest.

You listen with curiosity to their voices.

You copy the noises they make with their mouths.

First, you just make babbling sounds.

Later, you join the sounds together to produce your first words.

And finally, you string words together in simple sentences, which get gradually more and more complex the more words and expressions you absorb.

The whole process is so natural, you don't even notice you're learning. It feels good to communicate with your loved ones, and they applaud your every attempt at learning to speak.

Enjoy these feelings of effortless and joyful communication. How do they feel in your body?

Can you amplify the feelings of wellbeing? Let them radiate out of you like an aura of warmth, ease, and love.

Language comes easy to you. It is fun and delightful. You are a natural.

Soak up these feelings for a few moments more, relishing the sensations of perfect self-acceptance, bliss, and ease.

Now, take this image of yourself as a baby and all these wonderful feelings associated with language learning and easeful communication, shrink it down really small, and place it in your heart.

Take a few long, deep breaths, while you focus on the presence of beautiful Baby You, who is always in your heart.

You can call on your inner baby's wisdom any time you're feeling insecure about your language learning abilities.

Baby You is within you. Baby You knows that it can be done (because they've already done it), and they know that it is easy, fun, and effortless when led by curiosity and openness. Remember that always.

When you're ready, count back from ten to one, and start to come back to the here and now.

Notice the contact with the surface you are resting on.

Move your fingers and your toes.

Become aware that you are returning to your normal state of alertness, feeling refreshed and relaxed, and with a newfound confidence in your language abilities. The answers are all within you. You can do this.

THE HEART AND THE EMOTIONS

"The heart has its own language.
The heart knows a hundred thousand ways to speak."

"El corazón tiene su propio lenguaje.
El corazón conoce cien mil maneras de hablar."

~ Rumi, 13th century poet

HEART OR MIND?

In my early twenties, I lived in Japan for three years, teaching English as an assistant in secondary schools in the Osaka area. In my very first term there, I had a fabulous co-teacher called Ukena-sensei, and together we spent our days teaching 12-year-olds who had never learnt English before.

I would talk in simple English, engaging the kids in conversation (with lots of miming!), and Ukena-sensei would repeat back everything I said in Japanese. This worked well for the kids to get them used to listening to English, and it was also brilliant immersion for me in Japanese, which may have subconsciously been my reason for creating my bilingual immersion podcast, The Heartful Spanish Podcast, some twenty-five years later.

Anyway, the reason I mention this is that I remember being shocked one day when I said a sentence using the word "mind" and Ukena-sensei translated it as "*kokoro*", which I knew meant "heart" in Japanese. He even touched his hand on his heart. Whaat?!

Years later, I learnt that this is common to other Asian languages too. Here's what Jon Kabat-Zinn has to say about it:

> *"In Asian languages, the word for 'mind' and the word for 'heart' are the same. So if you're not hearing mindfulness in some deep way as heartfulness, you're not really understanding it. Compassion and kindness towards oneself are intrinsically woven into it. You could think of mindfulness as wise and affectionate attention"*
> *(Szalavitz, 2012).*

On a similar note, the spiritual teacher Mooji said these wise and soothing words: "Bring your mind into your heart, and the world will not trouble you" (Mooji, 2021).

A kind of softening occurs when we bring our mind into our heart, a quietening of the egoic self. I believe that leaning into this softening—allowing ourselves to be guided by our heart's wisdom—is the key to living a fulfilled life and showing up as our best selves, moment to moment. And the same applies to language learning; if we want to become fluent quickly and easily, it's essential to ignore the mind's ego chatter (or, better still, notice it and intentionally "soften"), letting ourselves be guided instead by the joy in our heart. Over the following pages, I'll show you how.

MINDFULNESS, THE EMOTIONS, AND LANGUAGE LEARNING

The word "mindfulness" is often translated in Spanish as "*plena atención*" meaning "full attention". If you're familiar with mindfulness practice, you'll know it's all about training in present-moment awareness, slowing down, and paying "full attention" to the world around you and to the feelings and sensations in your body. Mindfulness is proven to have positive effects on the brain, aiding concentration and cognitive function, deepening intuition and insight, and improving mood and emotional wellbeing (see Riopel, 2019).

Mindfulness practice is the antidote to the fast-paced, superficial lifestyle most of us live today, which has led more and more of us to experience unhappiness or mental health challenges. Our constant busyness and the need to be always "doing" or "striving" often mask our "numbing out" of difficult emotions and experiences. But emotions are our teachers, and if we bypass them or numb them out, we won't learn the important lessons they are here to teach us. Life will keep on providing us with more opportunities to learn those same lessons until we finally sit up and take notice. (Usually, this happens in a not-very-pleasant, bash-you-around-the-head way, through some kind of life crisis. And we don't want that, do we?)

So, what does this have to do with language learning? Well, I know I'm going to sound like a broken record here, but I cannot stress enough that *full engagement with the emotions and the senses is essential for fast, easy, and successful language learning.* And therein lies the connection between the practice of mindfulness and immersion-based, heart-led language learning. If you can be present to touch, smell, taste, hear, or see the things you are learning to talk about in Spanish (as well as feeling all the emotions those senses provoke in you), it will cement the words in your vocabulary much more quickly and lastingly than if you just learnt them two-dimensionally via a language app or a textbook.

This is because engagement with the emotions and the senses is closely linked to memory and reinforces the way we learn (see Tyng et al., 2017). Rather than just cognitive or theoretical learning, we gain a deeper, more experiential understanding this way. A mindful, emotions-based approach to languages creates new neural pathways that merely reading words on a page or screen cannot produce (see Lardone et al., 2018). As the old saying goes, "Tell me and I forget; teach me and I remember; involve me and I learn."

The more we practise the Spanish language in this engaged, mindful, heart-led way, the easier it will be for us to remember the new words and expressions we come across, and the sooner we'll start to feel fluent.

HEART ENERGY

Our hearts hold deep wisdom and beautiful, loving energy, and our lives would be so much easier if only we could practise getting "out of our heads and into our hearts" more often. In our heads, we are often led by fear, worry, and "what-ifs"—the default voice of our ego, our learned patterns. When we live from our hearts, our experience is more expansive, and we are loving, compassionate, and magnanimous. We are one with our wise inner self and the innately open, self-accepting, curious mindset we had as babies.

The easiest way to experience heart energy is to think back to one of the most profoundly beautiful emotional experiences of your life—a deeply loving connection or a moment of great joy, perhaps. Close your eyes and revisit that moment in your life, trying to relive all the feelings as vividly as possible. What are the sensations in your body? How does it feel in your heart area? Spend a few minutes savouring these elevated emotions, and enjoy reliving the bodily experience and expansive energy of your joyful or loving moment from the past. This is heart energy, and we can tap into it any time we choose.

The more we practise getting in tune with our heart energy, the more connected we will be to our best, most conscious selves, and the easier our connection and communication with others will be. We have all the answers within; we just have to slow down and listen.

When I first learnt about heart energy and experienced its power, I knew this was something I wanted to keep as a daily or multiple-times-daily ritual to keep me present to my best self, more often throughout the day. I loved it so much I even named my podcast after it. Follow your heart, and life will unfold beautifully before you. And the same principle applies in language learning, as we'll explore later.

HEART ENERGY AND COMMUNICATION

When we proactively choose to connect with our heart energy prior to communicating with our loved ones or before a conversation we anticipate could be difficult, we can call up our best, most loving self, and the result will be greatly improved communication, harmony, and ease.

And that's where it comes in handy for our language practice. Any time you have to make a phone call in Spanish or face a situation that could potentially cause you to feel nervous or worried about your speaking or comprehension skills, spend a few moments prior to the interaction focusing on the energy of your heart, to quieten the voice of your inner critic and bring you back into alignment with the best, most eloquent, and coherent version of yourself, trusting that the words you need will come to you.

This technique is great for ensuring optimum understanding and communication between two (or more) people. And if they taught it in schools, the world would be a better place.

MINI HEART ENERGY INFUSIONS THROUGHOUT YOUR DAY

This is a fantastic one-minute technique, a mini version of the previous exercise. It can be used in life in general or, in our case, specifically applied to the language learning situation.

Get into the habit of taking regular pauses throughout your day, whenever you remember—or when you are about to change activity or location, or you're about to interact with someone new—to infuse your whole being with the loving energy of your heart.

It is a super simple trick but a very powerful way to live more in alignment with your wisest, most loving self.

Try this before you practise your Spanish or every time you start a new chapter or exercise, and notice how the energy around your interactions and experiences changes.

Let's do it now. All you have to do is pause for a moment and drop into a place of deep stillness, knowingness, or oneness. (You might call this your inner calm, your higher self, your divine spark, consciousness, or connection to God, source or love, whatever works for you.)

Simply place an intention or a wish into your heart, breathe into it, and watch the magic unfold.

Here are some examples of intentions you could try:
- ♥ *I intend to experience fun and joy in my Spanish practice today.*
- ♥ *I wish to learn with curiosity and openness.*
- ♥ *I am choosing ease and flow now.*
- ♥ *I am open.*

Or a one-word version:
- ♥ *Joy*
- ♥ *Ease*
- ♥ *Flow*

You don't even need words for this one; you can just set a wordless intention, connecting to the feelings you wish to experience.

Try it. It's powerful. And super easy.

AFFIRMATION POWER

"Language creates reality. Words have power.
Speak always to create joy."

*"El lenguaje crea la realidad. Las palabras tienen poder.
Habla siempre para crear dicha."*

~ Deepak Chopra, Indian-American author

HOW AFFIRMATIONS WORK

Have you used positive affirmations before in your life? We are all affirming things the whole time, whether consciously and positively or subconsciously and (often) negatively. As humans, our brains are naturally wired towards negativity, so the chances are that if you don't make a conscious effort to use positive affirmations on a daily basis, your default thoughts may often be a running commentary on the problems in your life and worries about what's not going well.

In psychology, this is known as the negativity bias (Moore, 2019); it served a purpose for the survival and evolution of humans in the past. Today, however, we no longer need to be in constant "fight or flight" mode, because most of our modern-day fears are not immediate life-or-death situations, and it can be very draining and self-defeating to allow our mind to focus on them as if they were. But with intention and focus, we can find a better way—by affirming what we want in our lives instead.

From neuroscience, we know that the reticular activating system (RAS) in the brain filters out all the information we don't need to be constantly aware of in our daily lives and shows us more of what we intend to focus on (Rothstein & Stromme, n.d.). In simple terms, the functioning of the RAS means that *what we focus on grows* in our awareness and experience, a concept that is very similar to the law of attraction in spiritual or New Age thought.

My first awareness of the RAS (although I didn't know the name for it back then) came when I was looking to buy my first car, back in 1999. I ran my finger down the list of second-hand car ads in the newspapers, decided I wanted a Ford Fiesta, and suddenly there were Ford Fiestas all around me on the streets, wherever I looked! I'm sure you'll have experienced something similar at some point in your life.

We can put the RAS to good use in any area of life, by using affirmations to focus our minds on positive thoughts and outcomes in place of the default negativity we humans have a tendency towards. Instead of allowing our mind to ruminate on our problems and fears, we can make a conscious decision to affirm the things we want more of, and suddenly we start to see those things materialise "magically" in our lives. It's a powerful shift that occurs through setting intentions, using positive affirmations to change the focus of our thoughts, and taking small, feel-good actions in the direction of our goals.

Whether you believe in the law of attraction or not, at the very least you'll agree that turning the focus of your brain toward positive thoughts is a more easeful way to go through life.

AFFIRMATIONS TO SUPERCHARGE YOUR SPANISH

Just as in life itself, it's the same with language learning. When we hit a plateau or a tough spot or lose our motivation altogether, the negativity kicks in, and the things we say to ourselves can often take us plunging further into the abyss of despair and impossibility.

For example, our predominant thoughts about our Spanish may sound something like this:

- △ I don't have the time to study Spanish, so I never make progress.
- △ I'll never be fluent. It's so hard.
- △ I'm feeling completely unmotivated to learn Spanish.
- △ I find it really hard to remember new vocab.
- △ I don't understand grammar, and I hate it.
- △ My Spanish has stagnated.
- △ Language classes are boring.
- △ I feel so embarrassed when I have to speak Spanish. I should know more by now.

One of the most effective treatments for depression or anxiety is cognitive behavioural therapy (CBT, Beck, 2020). In CBT, patients learn to reframe their negative thoughts and replace them with more positive ones, which helps them create a mindset that feels better and enables them to take action to improve their situation. Applying this logic to our language learning, we can easily turn each of the previous negative thoughts on its head to affirm the opposite, and this simple shift will help us to feel better about our Spanish skills and practice.

The new replacement thoughts could look something like this:

- *I choose to dedicate a small amount of time every day/week to studying Spanish, and I'm noticing the progress I'm making.*
- *I'm taking small steps towards becoming fluent, and it's starting to feel easier for me.*
- *I'm noticing that Spanish is coming more easily to me. It feels good to be making progress.*
- *I'm feeling excited and motivated to learn Spanish by immersion in small doses.*
- *I now find it easier to remember the new vocab I hear and learn because I'm interested, open, and curious.*
- *I am absorbing grammar naturally by osmosis, and I love seeing how much more naturally it's coming to me.*
- *My Spanish is improving now as I practise in tiny doses often.*
- *I am finding new ways of learning real Spanish, and I'm actually finding it fun!*
- *I feel calm and confident when I speak Spanish. I am doing so much better than I was before.*

Often, it's too much of a stretch for us to affirm the opposite of our dominant negative thoughts, which is why I've included some "halfway point" affirmations whereby you affirm that you're on the way, making progress, noticing tiny improvements, or taking small steps in the right direction.

Affirmations have to feel good, and you have to be invested in them emotionally, so they must feel believable and realistic to you. This is the key to success, so make sure the words you use in your affirmations really resonate with your own unique situation and personality.

WRITE DOWN YOUR FEEL-GOOD AFFIRMATIONS

Use this space to write your own affirmations that feel good to you, creating your own versions of the ones in this section.

PERSONAL PRAYER OR AFFIRMATION OF OPENNESS TO POSSIBILITY

This exercise will be easier if you already have a spiritual practice, some kind of belief system—whether spiritual faith or simply a deep trust that things always work out well—and an understanding and experience of the law of attraction and manifesting. However, anyone can do this, regardless of beliefs. All that is needed is an attitude of openness to the possibility that your visualisation could come true.

If you have spiritual beliefs, try this simple prayer:

♥ *Please, Universe/God/Source/[insert object of your belief here], help me to make great progress with my Spanish with masses of ease, fun, and joy.*

For atheists, agnostics, or anyone averse to saying it like a prayer, just be open to the possibility that change is on its way. Try saying this affirmation instead:

♥ *I am open to the possibility that I can make great progress with my Spanish with masses of ease, fun, and joy.*

You can change the wording to suit you. Everyone is different, and it's important that the statement feels right to you.

For even more clarity, or for results that are more specific to your particular circumstances, refer back to your affirmations/visualisations in the first two exercises—Set an intention for your Spanish (on p.29) and Visualise your big picture goal (on p.32)—and adapt your words accordingly.

Write your personal prayer or affirmation of openness to possibility here:

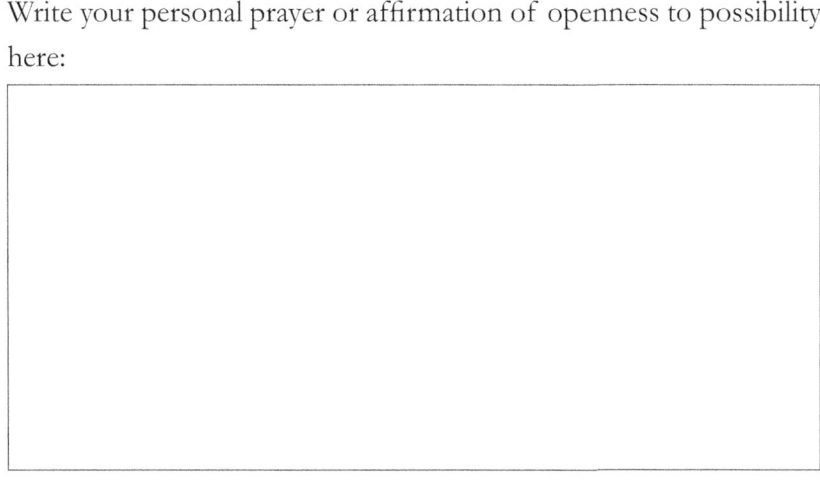

Commit to 30 days of saying this prayer or affirmation morning and night, and for extra oomph (if you feel like it), any time that you remember throughout the day.

>  **Top tip**
>
> To supercharge your affirmation practice, you could try pairing it with movement (e.g., doing some simple stretches or going for a run or a swim).

A POWERFUL AFFIRMATIONS HACK

This is *the* most powerful of all the self-help techniques I know. And if you only choose one new mindset hack from this workbook, let it be this one.

First thing in the morning when you wake up and last thing at night before you drop off are the two best times for placing affirmations and prayers into your subconscious mind, because when we're in the state between wakefulness and sleep, our brain is relaxed and our subconscious mind is most open to suggestion.

All you have to do is say your affirmations as you lie in bed before you go to sleep. It can be helpful to have a small note with your chosen words on by your bedside to remind you.

And if you're exhausted at bedtime, you can simplify your affirmation or prayer right down to just a one-word mantra repeated three times. Try saying, "*ease, ease, ease*", "*joy, joy, joy*", or "*fun, fun, fun*". Whatever words you feel most called to use.

If you're interested in hearing more, the second episode of my podcast is on this very subject. It's The Heartful Spanish Podcast, Season 1, Episode 2: The Bedtime Sweet Spot. Have a listen and see if this simple trick works for you.

WRITE DOWN YOUR PERSONAL PRAYER OR AFFIRMATION

It can be very powerful to write your personal prayer or affirmation in a journal. There's something magical about writing affirmations that reinforces them in your subconscious and makes them come to fruition quickly and effortlessly. (That doesn't mean you don't take action. You will but in an inspired, intuitive way that doesn't need to feel heavy or hard.)

You could also write your personal prayer or affirmation on a card and place it somewhere you'll see it often every day.

I have just written myself some post-it notes to place around the house saying, "I am a successful, published author", to help me push through the fears and procrastination and do what it takes to get this little workbook out in the world. If you are holding it in your hands right now, dear reader, then I consider my cheesy little notes to have been worth it.

ANCHOR YOUR PERSONAL PRAYER, AFFIRMATION, OR MANTRA TO A TRIGGER OR SYMBOL

Another helpful trick is to anchor your personal prayer, affirmation, or mantra to a trigger—for example, going up or down the stairs, stopping at a traffic light or roundabout, or boiling the kettle—to remind you to practise. Choose something that you do often. That way, you get lots of reminders throughout your day.

An image or symbol can be a potent addition to inspire you and fire you up with the elevated emotions that your fluency dream stirs in you. You could choose a flower, a leaf, or the sky, so every time you see the thing you've chosen, it serves as a reminder to whisper your affirmation or prayer to yourself. You can always just silently intend it or the one-word version of it. Another option is to choose a colour as a reminder, so for example, every time you see something blue (or yellow, etc.), you remember to practise your mantra.

> ☺ **Top tip**
>
> With all of these exercises, the more fun and light it feels, the better it will work, so choose what feels fabulous and enjoyable to you and let go of anything that doesn't resonate.
>
> If you find yourself getting frustrated with the repeated returning to the Your Vision section, please know that the reason for covering this so thoroughly is to cement your fluency dream firmly into your subconscious. This is important because it needs to be clearer in your mind than your previous default patterns. However, rather than doing it all in one go, a lighter option might be to skim-read the workbook and come back later to do these exercises one per day. Mark your calendar with some dedicated "My Fluency Vision" time each day, and don't let yourself off the hook.

GRATITUDE

"If the only prayer you ever say in your entire life is thank you, it will be enough."

"Si la única oración que dices en toda tu vida es gracias, será suficiente."

~ Meister Eckhart, 13th century philosopher

A WORD ON THE POWER OF GRATITUDE

Practising gratitude has been found to have multiple benefits for mental and emotional wellbeing (see Sansone & Sansone, 2010), so it's a powerful game changer for getting the results you want in any area of life. If you have ever done any kind of gratitude practice before, no doubt you'll have experienced it for yourself. Gratitude helps you focus on all the good that's already in your life and opens you up to allowing more of it in.

ADVANCE GRATITUDE

After reading *The Magic* by Rhonda Byrne and doing the exercises in the book every day for a short time with an online community I belong to, I have seen that it works—mind-blowingly well—to have gratitude in advance for what I want to attract into my life.

When it comes to language learning, giving gratitude in advance can be a powerful way to release the energy of feeling blocked or stagnated and open your mind to focus instead on the energy of the outcomes you want to achieve and especially the feelings you want to feel when you've achieved your goals.

There are a number of advance gratitude exercises we can do to improve our Spanish. You can choose any of the previous exercises and apply gratitude to the exercise *as if it were already your reality*.

When practising gratitude with any of these exercises, *it's super important for your dreams to feel realistic to you*, so choose your words carefully, finding a halfway point that feels more easily achievable if necessary. You can always revisit your objectives periodically to stretch your goals as you progress.

> ☺ **Top tip**
>
> Add the words "thank you, thank you, thank you" to the end of all of these advance gratitude exercises for added gratitude power.

ADVANCE GRATITUDE FOR YOUR INTENTIONS

Re-read your intentions from page 29 of this workbook and rewrite them here in the present tense, *as if they were your reality*, expressing gratitude. Write *why* you are grateful and include as much detail and emotion as possible.

Example:

- ♥ *I'm so grateful because I am starting to notice myself remembering more of the new words I learn, and I am feeling more positive and relaxed about my Spanish.*

ADVANCE GRATITUDE FOR YOUR VISION

Next, revisit the scenario and feelings involved in your big picture goal from page 32 of this workbook and rewrite them here in the present tense, expressing gratitude as if it were already true. The stronger the feelings you evoke, the more powerfully you will cement your vision in your subconscious mind.

Example:

- ♥ *I am deeply appreciative of the new opportunities that my improved Spanish is bringing me. I am starting to feel happier and more confident speaking in Spanish, and I'm having heaps more fun now.*

ADVANCE GRATITUDE FOR YOUR PERSONAL PRAYER OR AFFIRMATION

Now, go back to your personal prayer or affirmation of openness to possibility on page 55 and rewrite it here in the present tense, adding gratitude *because it's on its way.*

Example:

♥ *Thank you for the progress I am now making as I improve my Spanish with lots more ease, fun, and joy.*

BUSTING THROUGH YOUR BLOCKS

"Every problem has a solution; it may sometimes just need another perspective."

"Todo problema tiene una solución; a veces puede que solo necesite otra perspectiva."

~ Katherine Russell, author of NLP For Rookies

A WORD ABOUT BLOCKS

We all have blocks in different areas of our lives. They are our limiting beliefs—the stories we tell ourselves over and over again in our subconscious mind that hold us back from achieving our goals. We argue for our limitations, focusing on our weaknesses instead of our strengths and on perceived obstacles instead of potential solutions.

It's time to stop all that, and the first step is to identify our blocks. These will be different for everybody, but in this section, I've identified nine common blocks that may be holding you back from becoming fluent in Spanish.

Grab a pencil and underline the blocks that are relevant to you. Then, turn to the appropriate section and complete the exercises I've created to help you remove your blocks.

The number one block—and one that is common to many language learners—is believing that you "don't have time to learn Spanish". This classic lie becomes a self-fulfilling prophecy that holds a lot of people back from making progress. And I should know, because I've been saying it to myself for years, but in relation to my (now very rusty) Japanese.

The second block I've identified is not wanting to spend money on learning Spanish. Perhaps you've spent a lot of money (and time) on Spanish lessons in the past, and you don't feel it was money well invested. Whatever reasons you may have for not wanting to spend money, you'll soon see there are plenty of ways around this.

The third block is that "the vocab never seems to stick". You learn new words, but they don't seem to make it into your long-term memory, which reinforces the feeling of stagnation and lack of progress.

Block number four is the feeling that you "never get the chance to talk to native speakers". And this can even be a block for you if you live in the country, which happened to me when I lived in Lisbon, as a 19-year-old undergrad at a Portuguese university. If I could go back and whisper into shy, nervous, 19-year-old me's ear, I'd tell her: "You make the opportunities, my love. Now, go out and make friends."

Blocks number five and six are both about feelings of embarrassment around speaking Spanish—feeling embarrassed to make mistakes and feeling embarrassed about having a strong accent. I never had this problem in the past, because I have a fairly good ear and ability to mimic native speakers and making mistakes wasn't a big concern of mine. But when I started my podcast and accompanying Instagram account a couple of years ago, I suddenly became hyper-aware of all the non-native-sounding words and phrases that came out of my mouth! (It's all about where you put your focus, see?) I've never felt more blocked and "un-fluent" in my life—ironic considering I was creating a podcast to help people find ease and flow in their language learning!

Just to be clear, I don't know any less Spanish than when I started my podcast. In fact, I probably know more now; it's just that my flow has been a bit blocked by me focusing on mistakes—and obsessively trying not to make any!—instead of simply feeling ease and flow when speaking Spanish (which was my previous default mode). This example demonstrates why traditional methods that focus on accumulating vocabulary and perfecting sentence structures are not the answer when it comes to actually gaining fluency.

The seventh block relates to not being able to get motivated to practise or study Spanish. And this happens to all of us at times, so make sure you come back to this one any time your joyful language practice falls by the wayside.

The eighth block is a particularly blocky block(!), and it relates to not being able to understand native speakers and having the feeling that it's all way over your head. This is a perfectly normal phase in language learning, my lovely, and it doesn't have to keep you stuck.

Finally, the ninth block relates to all the different variations on the theme of "I can't do this". These include, but are not limited to, the following limiting beliefs: "It's too difficult", "I'm no good at languages", or "I'm too old/stupid/lazy/ [insert limiting belief of preference] to learn Spanish".

Read on, my friend, for the Heartful Spanish way to bust through all of these common and completely normal blocks on the road to fluency.

BUSTING THROUGH BLOCK #1. "I DON'T HAVE TIME TO LEARN SPANISH."

I get it; you're busy. You have countless obligations and very little free time. But I promise you, even if you're a time-poor mum of a newborn baby, you can find a way to make progress on your Spanish. You just have to want it enough.

In her TED talk on time management, expert Laura Vanderkam points out that saying "I don't have time" is often another way of saying "It's not a priority for me". And 2,600 years before TED talks existed, Chinese philosopher Lao Tzu said, "Time is a created thing. To say 'I don't have time', is like saying 'I don't want to'".

Now try saying, "I don't want to learn Spanish" and "Spanish is not a priority for me" instead. Take a moment and see how that feels in your body. I'm guessing the first statement is not true for you, or you wouldn't be reading this workbook. The second one might resonate more with how you really feel. And I'm here to tell you that it's perfectly OK if Spanish isn't your number one priority.

In order to improve your fluency, you just have to set the intention to dedicate some time to practising more often (even if just five minutes a day a few times a week is all you can manage as a baseline).

We all have 24 hours in a day, but some people seem to manage to fit a heck of a lot into their days, whereas others don't manage to make much progress at all. (Zero judgement from me; I've been in the latter camp most of my life!) Be kind to yourself, first and foremost, but take a long, honest look at the benefits of increasing your fluency versus the reasons why you're staying stagnated. With the help of the next two exercises, you'll be able to identify and unravel the patterns that have got you stuck.

BRAINSTORM THE BENEFITS IMPROVED SPANISH FLUENCY WOULD BRING YOU

In case you need some inspiration regarding the benefits that learning Spanish can bring, these could include more fun, better communication with Spanish speakers, new and improved friendships, more opportunities for work or business, feeling proud of yourself for mastering a new skill, feeling more at home in Spain or Latin America, or feeling good about yourself for breaking through the language barrier.

And let's not forget the brain benefits of speaking more than one language, such as improved attention and focus (Kovács & Mehler, 2009), as well as protection against age-related decline and dementia (Liu & Wu, 2021).

What benefits can you think of for your specific situation and life dreams? Write them in the left-hand column of this table. Then, on the right, explore the feelings these benefits would bring you.

Future situation: increased fluency	
Benefits	**How this would make me feel**
Example: If I became more fluent in Spanish, I would be able to communicate with Spanish speakers easily and effortlessly. / I would make more friends, have more fun and be happier. / I would have more business (or work) opportunities. / I would feel confident backpacking around Spain or Latin America.	*I would feel accomplished, connected, confident, able, independent, calm, and proud of myself for learning a new skill.*

Here's some more space to explore the benefits that improved fluency would bring you and how it would make you feel.

Future situation: increased fluency	
Benefits	**How this would make me feel**

CONSIDER THE REASONS YOU'RE STAYING STUCK

You've identified the benefits that improved fluency would bring you. Now, how about the reasons why you're staying stuck? These can be more difficult to identify, as they're often buried deep in your subconscious. So, some digging around may be required for this exercise. Here are a few questions to get you started:

What's stopping you from making progress? What are the subconscious "benefits" for you of staying stuck? Maybe it's easier to stop trying and let someone else do the speaking than to push through the discomfort of making mistakes, sounding foreign, or feeling stupid.

Newsflash: making mistakes and sounding foreign are both an integral part of learning a language. Feeling stupid is optional. The trick is to be more accepting of our flaws and push on anyway, and then speaking Spanish becomes more of a fun challenge on our journey to fluency than a torturous obligation to be avoided at all costs.

Look at the reasons you've identified one by one, write them down in the table below, and see how they are making you feel. Here's where the honesty comes in. It may be that the choices you're making, moment to moment, are bringing you short-term benefits but long-term pain and frustration.

For example, "A benefit of staying stuck is that I don't have to tackle uncomfortable situations—I can always find someone to help me or to translate for me." Now, look at that statement a little closer and see how it feels to always "need" someone to help you or translate for you.

Current situation: staying stuck	
Reasons for staying stuck	**How this makes me feel**
Examples: It's easier this way. / I can always find someone to help me. / I can muddle through. / Tom always translates for me, so I don't have to worry about feeling stupid or be embarrassed about making mistakes in front of him. / I don't have to spend time doing Spanish exercises or lessons. / I don't have to make an effort.	*Helpless, useless, dependent, not very competent, needy, complacent, frustrated, embarrassed, not very accomplished, "blocked", self-critical, limited in what I can do, lacking in self-discipline, not reaching my full potential…*

Here's some more space to explore the reasons why you're staying stuck and see how they are making you feel.

Current situation: staying stuck	
Reasons for staying stuck	**How this makes me feel**

CHECK IN WITH YOUR BODY WISDOM

Read through those feelings you expressed in the right-hand column of the previous table. How does it feel in your body to read those words? Where do you feel it? Does it feel like the best version of you? Write down anything you observe and any "ahas" that spring to mind.

LET GO OF THE NEGATIVE FEELINGS FROM YOUR CURRENT SITUATION

Negative emotions are just a signal that things are not as we'd like them to be. So, thank your body for giving you that information. Now it's time to let those feelings go and choose different ones instead. It really can be that simple. Don't try so hard. Just smile, feel your energy shift, and choose a better-feeling thought instead.

Here are a few simple words you could say to yourself to accompany this shift:

- ♥ *I choose ease.*
- ♥ *I choose joy.*
- ♥ *I choose flow.*

KEEP A FOCUS AND INTENTION LOG

A simple trick for gaining awareness on how you're using your time and where your focus is going is to use a focus and intention log. (I used to call it a "time log", but "focus and intention log" puts it in a more positive light and says more clearly what I want it to do.)

I do this on a blank sheet of paper, divided into three columns like this:

Time	Focus & intention	Notes / Things to come back to
9:18	Write blog post with ease and flow	Felt (and ignored) the urge to check social media. Yay!
10:05	Translate article with joy and gratitude	Remembered I need to call Mum later.
11:38	Draft podcast episode, remembering my 'why' (to help people believe in themselves and their ability to learn languages)	Look up Lao Tzu quote about complicating life

At random times throughout the day, usually when I'm changing activity or taking a break, I write down the time, what I'm going to focus on next, along with an intention for how I want to feel or why I am choosing to focus on that. Then I use the third column for anything that arises while I'm focusing that I want to remember later or learn from, plus any "shiny object" distractions that could take me away from my object of focus. I can come back to the third column later, once I've accomplished my goal.

If you complete a focus and intention log for a few whole days, checking in as often as you remember, you'll get a good idea of when you're using your time consciously and when you're not doing so great on that front.

Two other helpful tools for staying focused and using your time well are productivity apps (like Nirvana or Trello) for organising your priorities and online accountability groups or platforms, which I talk more about in the section on building consistency.

☺ **Top tip**

To go the extra mile, you could set alarms to remind yourself to check in with your focus and intention log at regular intervals. Or, if you wear an activity band or smart watch on your wrist, does it give you regular reminders when you've been sitting for too long? Those would be great nudges to remind you to check back in with your focus and intentions.

To add a bit of energetic magic, you could combine this practice with mini heart energy infusions, as described earlier on page 45, by simply breathing and focusing on your intention for the next segment of your day every time you check in.

IDENTIFY YOUR TIME SUCKS AND POTENTIAL SOLUTIONS OR REPLACEMENTS

Now identify the time sucks in your life. Maybe you watch a couple of Netflix episodes every evening, or you spend half an hour more than you'd like to on social media each day. Where could you cut down on unnecessary time wasting or activities that aren't taking your life in the direction you'd like it to go?

Use the box below to capture your thoughts on your habitual time sucks and how they make you feel, and then identify potential replacements for them that would help you with your Spanish learning. This isn't about taking away all your leisure time, just replacing (or partially replacing) some activities that may not be leading you toward the outcomes you want with other, more ultimately fulfilling ones. And it doesn't have to be a lot—in fact, it's best to start really small with new habits, say just five minutes at a time. And if that feels like too much, try two minutes. Easy wins help you build good habits.

Time suck	What's going on?	Potential solution (or replacement)
Social media	*I spend way too much time scrolling on Facebook and Instagram (about two hours every day), and I always feel annoyed with myself afterwards.*	*I could limit my time use to, say, 30 mins after lunch, and set an alarm so I know when I have to switch off. I could spend some of the extra time practising my Spanish in a way that feels fun and light.*
Netflix	*I watch two episodes of a Netflix series most nights after dinner, and I usually end up getting to bed too late.*	*I could reduce my viewing time (either just watch one episode per night or limit it to three or four nights per week). I could enjoy an earlier night and read a Spanish book in bed.*

COMBINE YOUR FAVOURITE TIME SUCKS WITH YOUR SPANISH PRACTICE

Both of the classic time sucks mentioned in the previous subsection (Netflix and social media) would be perfect pastimes to combine with your Spanish learning. You could watch Spanish or Latin American programmes on Netflix (or your favourite ones in English, but with the Spanish subtitles on), or you could follow language teachers or native Spanish speakers that appeal to you on Instagram. (I'll go into this in more detail later, in the Bringing in the Joy Factor section.)

It's really important to do any potentially mindless screen-related activities in a mindful way though, setting the intention to have fun and improve your Spanish each time you open up the app or press play. Be sure to jot down any new vocab that captures your curiosity.

Use the box below to brainstorm ways to link your favourite time sucks to your Spanish learning. I've included a couple of examples for you.

Time suck	What's going on?	Ways to combine it with your Spanish practice
Instagram	I spend way too much time on Instagram (about an hour every day), and it feels unfulfilling. I know it's holding me back from being my best self.	I could follow some Spanish language teachers on Instagram (e.g., @espanol_con_guada, @hablaconellas, or @spanishwithelisabeth) and keep a notebook nearby to jot down any new or useful expressions I learn.
TV	I watch a lot of Netflix, HBO, Amazon Prime, etc. but I love it so much!	I could watch a Spanish or Latin American series (e.g., "La casa de papel" or "Vis a vis" on Netflix) or even a series I love in English but with Spanish subtitles on. (This could be the perfect excuse to watch an old favourite again.)

BUSTING THROUGH BLOCK #2:
"I DON'T WANT TO SPEND MONEY ON LEARNING SPANISH."

Aha! This one, my friend, is no longer a block in today's globalised digital society, so you can cross it off your list right now. There are *so* many ways you can increase your exposure to the Spanish language without spending a penny on lessons. There are also thousands of excellent Spanish teachers giving away tons of free content online. All you need to do is choose the ones that resonate with you—fabulous content, an accent/voice you can understand, clear explanations, whatever appeals to you—and up your game.

Use this box to explore ways in which you can deepen your Spanish learning using free online content. Think YouTube, podcasts, Instagram, maybe even TikTok if that feels like fun to you. Also consider any streaming media services or pay television networks you're already subscribed to, like HBO, Amazon Prime Video, Netflix, etc.

For more inspiration, check out the Resources for your Spanish section at the end of this workbook.

Ways I can improve my Spanish for free
♥ *I could search on my podcast platform (e.g., Spotify, Apple Podcasts, etc.) or on YouTube for "Spanish" and related key word combinations ("learn Spanish", "speak Spanish", etc.) and check out the teachers that appeal to me.* ♥ *I could listen to podcasts such as Lightspeed Spanish, Notes in Spanish, Fluent Spanish Express, or (shameless plug!) The Heartful Spanish Podcast and make notes on any interesting new vocab that I hear.*

Here's a little more space for brainstorming ways you can improve your Spanish for free…

By the way, "upping your game" doesn't necessarily mean spending more time on studying Spanish. It's more about consistency and focusing your attention (which we will cover in the section on creating a strategy and plan), as well as finding ways to make it fun and to make the new vocabulary stick, which leads me onto the next block we're going to tackle.

BUSTING THROUGH BLOCK #3: "THE VOCAB NEVER SEEMS TO STICK."

I can totally relate to this block. Once you're fluent, it can be hard to keep increasing your vocab because you no longer feel the need to focus on learning the way you do earlier in your Spanish learning journey—you can get by fine without it. And when you stop needing to improve, you also stop focusing on learning new words and phrases, and guess what happens? Yep, you stop learning!

If you're experiencing this problem of vocab not sticking in your memory, whether you're a complete beginner, already fluent, or somewhere in between, here's a simple trick to increase your Spanish vocab and help it stick: start a feel-good Spanish notebook to keep up the joy factor.

START A JOYFUL VOCAB NOTEBOOK

This is a place to collect the new words and phrases you come across that spark your language joy (or at least your curiosity) and make you *want* to remember them. It's also a great way to ensure you notice your progress, which is key to keeping up the motivation and feeling good about your learning.

Even if you only jot down a couple of words or phrases a day a few times a week, over a month or a year it really starts to add up. And every time you look back at the words you've written down, you reinforce the learning process by noticing how much you've learnt. (Noticing your successes—no matter how small—creates a snowball effect of feel-good language learning, making you want to learn more. A virtuous cycle if you will.)

You can use a pocket-sized notebook or a lined exercise book, whatever works for you. When I first moved to Spain, I already had my Spanish degree and had lived in Mexico for a year, but I wanted to expand my vocab, so I kept a lined exercise book where I wrote down the new words that cropped up in my daily life.

I split it into three columns like this:

Spanish	English	Notes/Context
cotorrear	To rabbit on / blather on / chat away	From *cotorra* (parrot), which also means "chatterbox"
escurrir el bulto	To duck / wriggle out of something	"*Escurrir*" means "to slip/slide" (also "to pour"), "*bulto*" means "package" or "bulk"
para ti la perra gorda	Literally "the fat dog for you" but used to mean "Yeah, yeah, whatever."	(A funny expression used when you can't be bothered to argue any more)

These examples are actual entries from my blog, My Little Spanish Notebook, where I note down curious words and expressions that I come across in my daily life here in Spain and in my work as a translator. Interestingly, when I don't focus on blogging, I can go for weeks or months without hearing a new word, but whenever I decide to "up my game" and blog more regularly, fabulous words start popping up all over the place. (A similar thing happens with our native language too. You hear a new word that makes you sit up and pay attention, and then "magically" that same word appears a few times over the next few days in different contexts. It's the brain's RAS in action again, showing us more of what we decide to focus on.)

Try this in blog form, if you're so inclined, or otherwise a simple notebook will do fine. I'd love to hear how you get on and which words spark your language joy.

KEEP UP YOUR JOYFUL VOCAB HABIT AND KEEP IT FEELING GOOD

Nowadays, I tend to use my phone to jot down cool words and expressions that light up my fabulous vocab radar. Sometimes I use a pocket-sized notebook. Both of these options (phone or pocket notebook) are good because you can take them everywhere with you, which makes it easier to keep up the habit. That said, we all know the pitfalls of using a phone for something like this; we can easily get sucked in accidentally to a million and one other shiny things when we pick up our device. So, if you find the phone distracting, just go back to the good ol' pen and paper version.

Whenever you notice you've dropped the habit of collecting feel-good Spanish vocab (as most people will at some time or other), just forgive yourself and pick right back up where you left off. No big deal. It happens. We all forget about our good habits and intentions every now and again, sometimes for long stretches of time. Drop all idea of perfection and just focus on getting back on the horse. And congratulate yourself when you do.

This is the key to feel-good language learning. Beating ourselves up has no place here. Noticing you've fallen off the wagon is the first step. It may feel uncomfortable, and you might feel annoyed with yourself. Notice all those feelings too. It's all useful information that's showing you what you don't want and helping you gain clarity on what you do want instead.

Congratulate yourself whenever you log a new word or complete a page of your notebook. This gives you a dopamine hit that will feel good and contribute to rewiring your brain, creating the new neural pathways to reinforce the habit change. Reward yourself for your achievements, no matter how small. This will help you cement the habit of learning with curiosity and expanding your vocab.

USE FLASHCARDS OR AN APP

For added memory boosting, it's a great practice to transfer the words you want to remember from your feel-good Spanish vocab notebook to flashcards or an app like AnkiApp. This way, you can test yourself periodically (or get a friend or accountability partner to test you), and you'll ensure the words stick in your memory more easily.

I know this tip sounds really uninspiring, and it probably won't appeal to you unless you're aiming to take exams in Spanish, but it's a sure-fire way to improve your memory if you're finding that the new vocab you're learning isn't going in. Buy or make yourself some flashcards, or download the AnkiApp and see for yourself what a difference it makes.

BUSTING THROUGH BLOCK #4
"I NEVER GET THE OPPORTUNITY TO TALK WITH NATIVE SPEAKERS."

Oh, my lovely, if this is one of your big blocks, I hear you, because it's been a huge block of mine too (for the last 20 years or so, with the other languages I used to speak but am now very rusty in). However, I'm excited to tell you that you can cross this one off your list too, because with the technology we have today, it has never been easier to find a native speaker to chat to.

CONVERSATION EXCHANGE

A fantastic way to practise with a native speaker is to do a conversation exchange, where you spend half the time chatting in your native language and half the time chatting in your target language (in our case, Spanish).

There are numerous language exchange apps and online platforms that you can use for free. (Many of them also offer additional paid features.) This technology is a game changer, and it's one of the main reasons why it's no longer impossible to learn a language without going to the country. A good online language exchange app can create a safe, fun environment to learn in. (Obviously, do take the usual precautions regarding online safety when chatting with a stranger.)

Here are just a few of the many language exchange platforms that are out there.

Conversation exchange apps:
- HelloTalk
- Tandem
- Speaky

Conversation exchange websites:
- www.mylanguageexchange.com
- www.openlanguageexchange.com
- www.easylanguageexchange.com

The thing about language exchanges is that, like in life itself, there has to be a similar amount of give and take. You'll find that, just as in the real world, there are some people that are just "takers". (They only want to practise their target language and aren't keen to help you with yours.) In language learning—just as in life itself—avoid these types like the plague!

It might take some trial and error to find people you enjoy chatting to who are equally as happy to help you with your Spanish as they are to practise their English with you, but when you do, you've hit gold, and your language learning will improve exponentially because you'll be highly motivated to chat with your new friends.

Some of these apps and websites allow you to search by location in your local area to find a partner you could meet up with, which would add hugely to the fun factor if you find someone you get on well with. (Again, do be careful if you decide to meet in person with someone you met on the internet.)

Other conversation apps include the facility to correct your mistakes, to write to your partner like a pen pal, to take voice notes, or to translate words and phrases automatically within the app. Try a few until you find one you like.

With a language exchange, it's vital to create an atmosphere of openness and to be accepting of each other's mistakes. Also, learn to be OK with being corrected, or—even better—actively encourage it by asking your partner to correct you sometimes. On the other hand, don't go overboard correcting your partner's every single mistake, or they might get frustrated pretty quickly! Again, it's a case of *"prueba y error"* (trial and error) here until you find a level of correction you're both comfortable with. As always in heart-centred language learning, if it feels good, you're on the right track.

When you have a conversation partner you click with, a conversation exchange can be great fun, and you'll improve fast without even realising it. This is why everyone says total immersion is the best way to learn a language—because it usually happens in an atmosphere of fun and connection. But that can be the source of many mindset blocks and much self-criticism for the people who move to a Spanish-speaking country and—due to a mixture of circumstances and mindset blocks—don't find this to be the case. (If this is you, don't worry. We'll cover this in the next few exercises.)

NATIVE CONVERSATION TEACHERS

If you're short on time but are happy to pay a bit of money to practise speaking Spanish, there are tons of fabulous resources you can use today to book some time to chat with a native conversation teacher or a qualified language teacher. Less experienced/qualified teachers usually charge less, but that doesn't necessarily mean they are worse for your Spanish practice. Try a few until you find one (or more) that you like. This is feel-good language learning, remember, so it's super important to keep trying different teachers until you find one that you love or at least someone you enjoy chatting with.

Here are a few of the top platforms you can use to connect with online language teachers and practise your Spanish conversation.

- Italki www.italki.com
- Preply www.preply.com
- Verbalplanet www.verbalplanet.com

As with language exchange partners, finding a teacher you connect with can sometimes take a few attempts, but it's worth persevering, because once you have a teacher or a few teachers that you click with, your language will improve in no time, and you'll really want to keep going because you're enjoying yourself and having fun.

LANGUAGE PRACTICE WITH A BOT

Another way to get around the difficulty of finding someone to practise with is to take advantage of the new technologies and practise your Spanish with an AI (artificial intelligence) conversation partner, such as ChatGPT. The great thing about using AI for your language practice is that you can do as little or as much as you like, stopping whenever you get bored, and you can do it any time of the day or night at your convenience. You can also ask it to help you with words you don't understand, so it's like talking with a super patient, non-judgmental conversation partner and a dictionary in your hand. Give it a try and see if you find it helpful (and fun).

BUSTING THROUGH BLOCK #5: "I'M EMBARRASSED TO MAKE MISTAKES."

Aw, darling, if this is one of your blocks, welcome to the "embarrassed to look silly" club! Only the highest-evolved of humans actually *welcome* making mistakes, because they know that it's the best way to learn (in life and in languages). For the rest of us mere mortals, it can feel embarrassing, even excruciating, to have to talk in our imperfect accent whilst making tons of mistakes. The answer to this problem is that *the only way is through, my dear.*

PUSH THROUGH THE DISCOMFORT

You know what that means, don't you? Yep, you've just got to talk, talk, talk until it starts to feel natural to you. Keep on pushing yourself through the discomfort until speaking Spanish eventually stops being embarrassing for you. It's really worth persevering because as the discomfort disappears, your enjoyment level will increase, along with your self-confidence.

And this is a process that everyone goes through on their language learning journey. No one starts off speaking perfectly. Everyone makes mistakes at times, even fluent speakers. (More than you'd imagine, actually! As I mentioned earlier, fluency does *not* mean perfection; it means finding *flow* and no longer holding yourself back from expressing yourself freely.)

So, the next time you feel embarrassed to speak Spanish, just remember that on the other side of the discomfort is a more fluent, happier, more confident you. Notice the feelings of discomfort or embarrassment, give yourself extra amounts of love and kindness, and keep on trucking, my friend, because that discomfort is a sign that you're on the way to fluency. And it's a lot less painful than the discomfort and frustration of staying stuck.

Try these affirmations:

- *I am becoming more and more OK with not speaking perfect Spanish, and I'm learning to push on through anyway.*
- *I am learning to accept that making mistakes is part of learning languages, and I am starting to be more accepting of myself as I practise speaking Spanish.*
- *I am being kinder to myself as I practise speaking Spanish, and I am focusing on the improved feelings I am experiencing.*

HUSH (OR LEARN TO IGNORE) YOUR INNER CRITIC

Your inner critic is your worst enemy when you're trying to sound confident in a foreign language. You absolutely must let go of self-criticism and self-consciousness if you want to learn to speak more fluently. Because if you let your inner critic yada on as he or she likes to do, saying things like, "I don't know how to use the subjunctive", "I'm always making mistakes", or "I should speak better Spanish by now", I'm here to tell you *it will only get worse!* Why? Because that little voice in your head is sabotaging your every attempt to talk more fluently. That ol' meanie is holding you back every step of the way! It's like trying to ride a bike with the brakes on. Painful, slow, and bumpy, right?

A great trick that will help you hush (or learn to ignore) your inner critic is to start to *talk to yourself in Spanish out loud* as often as you can throughout your day. People who are naturally good at languages do this automatically when they first begin learning a new language. Sounds nuts, I know, but it really helps you get in the habit of pushing on through, even when you don't have all the words and expressions you need. Your inner critic will get used to you talking in Spanish and will eventually quieten down. For a short cut to this process, try the next exercise.

SUMMON UP YOUR INNER MOTIVATIONAL COACH

I know that sounds super cheesy, but the number one must-have if you want to become comfortable speaking a language is to *keep it feeling good and keep telling yourself you're doing* OK. Talk to yourself like you would talk to your best friend.

So, the next time you catch yourself thinking the self-critical thoughts you identified in the previous exercise, try doing the following:

1. Notice the voice of your inner critic and the mean words it says.
2. Pause and breathe.
3. Thank your inner critic.
4. Tell it it's no longer welcome around here.
5. Replace the thoughts with something kinder and more accepting instead.

Here are some examples of replacement thoughts your inner motivational coach might come up with:

- ♥ *"I am finding ways to express what I want to say, and it feels amazing!"*
- ♥ *"I'm learning new ways of saying things, and I'm proud of myself."*
- ♥ *"I am focusing on what I can say and understand, and I am starting to find ease and flow when I speak Spanish."*

Or, here are a few shorter ones for simplicity:

- ♥ *"I'm doing OK."*
- ♥ *"I'm focusing on communicating."*
- ♥ *"I'm doing better than before."*

ASK A NATIVE

If you're not sure how to say something in Spanish—and it's something you're curious about or you feel you need an answer for—you can always ask a native in this fabulous, globally connected day and age we live in. There are tons of online forums, websites, and apps for getting feedback from native speakers on your Spanish (or other language) questions and doubts. Just be aware that, like everything on the internet, you can't always guarantee the accuracy of the information, and often two linguists or even two native speakers will have differing opinions on the best way to translate something.

Here are three useful resources for getting answers from native speakers and linguists:

- Wordreference (forum)
- HiNative (app)
- Linguee (website)

BUSTING THROUGH BLOCK #6: "I'M EMBARRASSED ABOUT MY ACCENT."

Having a non-native accent is normal if you're not native (well, duh!), and it's perfectly OK, despite what your inner critic might have to say on the matter.

It's actually very rare—almost unheard of, in fact—for a non-native speaker, no matter how fluent, to sound like a native speaker consistently and in every instance. Think of your non-native English-speaking friends. A really good, fluent, non-native speaker may be able to pull it off for a short while, but tiredness or errors will eventually crop up at some point and give the game away that they're not native. It doesn't matter, of course, because you understand them just fine anyway. So, if sounding non-native has been causing you embarrassment, forget about perfection and just focus on improvement.

Here are a few ideas you can try to improve your accent a notch or two up the (imaginary) scale from "total *guiri/gringo*"[1] to "almost native-sounding".

> **Top tip**
>
> Remember, no one's actually measuring you on this made-up scale, my love. And if they are, f*** 'em. ('Scuse my language. Sorry, not sorry.)

SET THE INTENTION TO IMPROVE YOUR ACCENT

This may sound simplistic, but this is *the key step to sounding more like a native speaker* and one that many people skip. Intention is everything in language learning, as in life itself, so be sure to set a firm intention to improve your accent each time you work on it. You'll be surprised at how much you improve with just intention and attention alone. (The next couple of exercises cover the attention part.)

Try these affirmations:

- ♥ *I intend to improve my Spanish accent in a way that feels good by dedicating ___ minutes every week to focused practice.*
- ♥ *I am setting the intention to find ways to improve my accent in Spanish.*
- ♥ *My Spanish accent is starting to get better now.*

PRACTISE SPECIFIC SPANISH SOUNDS

At first, it may take a concerted effort to make your mouth create the same sounds that native speakers make, so just try to relax and have a bit of fun with it.

Notice the specific sounds in Spanish that are tricky for us English speakers: generally speaking, they are the sounds of the

---

1 "Guiri" is used in Spain to say (pejoratively or perhaps—although not often!—affectionately) "foreigner". "Gringo/gringa" is the Latin American equivalent.

letters r, j/g, ll, d, v, and c/z (this last one in Spain only; in Latin American Spanish, it's the same as the /s/ sound).

Here are some examples of words that include these sounds that are difficult to pronounce in Spanish for native English speakers. Try saying these words out loud. Exaggerate your Spanish accent as much as possible. Recordings of these words are available on Instagram at @heartfulspanishpodcast in my story highlights under "Pronunciation".

arroyo (stream, brook)

rabia (anger, frustration)

rojo (red)

cerrar (to close, to shut)

cerrado (closed, shut)

coger (to take, to catch)

feroz (fierce)

jardín (garden)

dedos (fingers, toes)

verdad (truth, true)

calle (street)

llave (key)

Now it's your turn!

Listen out for native speakers saying different words that contain the above letters/sounds. Ideally, use online materials or recordings that you can play over and over, so you can practise copying native pronunciation by repeating the words out loud. Choose words and sentences that appeal to you, ones you know will come in handy, or ones that are related to subjects you're interested in.

If you need a little extra help in this area, there are plenty of YouTube videos with language experts and accent coaches that can help you improve your pronunciation. To find out which specific sounds are the hardest for you, record yourself repeating a sentence after a native Spanish speaker and notice the elements that sound least like the original when you say them. Those are the parts you need to focus on to improve your pronunciation.

Check out Ruben from Linguistix, an expert on Spanish pronunciation who has lots of useful material on YouTube and on his website, www.linguistixpro.com/spanish.

LISTEN TO NATIVE SPEAKERS AND MIMIC THEIR ACCENTS

I realise I'm not telling you anything you don't know here. But how often do you actually dedicate time and effort to listening to native speakers and emulating what you hear? If your Spanish has stagnated and your English (or other native language) accent is very strong, the chances are it's because you've relaxed your focus in this area, so here's a simple outline of what you need to do to remedy this.

Find native Spanish speakers or teachers on your favourite platforms (e.g., YouTube, Instagram, podcast players, etc.). Choose ones you like the look and feel of and whose content and/or message resonates with you. Then, simply listen to them, using the pause and rewind functions as needed, and copy what they say, mimicking their accents and intonation as best you can.

I recommend you do this in small chunks so as not to get overwhelmed. Just choose short videos or audios and practise for a few minutes at a time at first.

> **Top tip**
>
> Exaggerate a little when you mimic native speakers' accents. Be prepared to have a laugh at yourself. But practise this often, and you'll soon improve your accent.

KEEP IT FEELING GOOD

Only do the last three exercises when it feels right to you or when you feel inspired to do them. (And that goes for all the exercises in this workbook.)

As always, keep in mind this guiding motto of feel-good language learning: LAMFO—Little Amounts, Fun, and Often. (I just made that up. Do you like it?) Now, "often" may mean five times a week if you're just starting out or if your accent needs considerable focus, but it may just mean once a week for this particular practice if that's what feels right to you. For often, read "consistently". (It's just that "consistently" doesn't make for such a fun acronym.)

BE KINDER TO YOURSELF

There are two exercises in Busting through Block #5 ("I'm embarrassed to make mistakes") that are also relevant if you're embarrassed about your accent. They are "Hush (or learn to ignore) your inner critic" on page 95 and "Summon up your inner motivational coach" on page 96. So, if you skipped that block before (or if you feel like repeating it with a focus on improving your accent), check out those two exercises, which are aimed to help you develop a kinder, more motivational inner voice to help you feel better as you focus on improving your language and mindset.

BUSTING THROUGH BLOCK #7
"I CAN'T GET MOTIVATED TO PRACTISE/ STUDY SPANISH."

A lack of motivation to practise or study Spanish is a common problem, especially if you've hit a plateau or you've been stagnating for a while. Is your vision strong enough? Are you being present to your "why"? How will you feel in five or ten years' time if you stay where you are? (If the answer is "It doesn't really bother me that much", then try going back to the visualisation practices at the beginning of this workbook, choose the ones that speak to you, and do them daily, or—better still—multiple times daily.)

And the most important question of all: Is your Spanish practice *fun* enough? Fun is the sure-fire way to fluency. Feeling bored or obligated, beating yourself up, or experiencing negative emotions only feeds the stagnation.

Journal on these questions here, digging deep into the "worst" and "best case scenarios" for your five- or ten-year outcomes, and see what comes up for you.

More space for reflecting on the reasons for your lack of motivation…

(Recap of prompts: Is your vision strong enough? Are you being present to your "why"? How will you feel in five or ten years' time if you stay where you are? Is your Spanish practice fun enough? Contemplate the "worst" and "best case scenarios" for your five- or ten-year outcomes.)

LIGHTEN THE ENERGY

If you've identified some uncomfortable feelings about the thought of being stuck where you are with your Spanish in ten years' time, it's time to make a concerted effort to lighten the energy.

The discomfort you've identified is a sign that your Spanish journey is not going as well as it could. A signpost, if you will, telling you to change track. Can you be present to the emotion in your body? Thank it for what it has revealed to you. Can you love the part of you that's been struggling? It's a part of you too and is therefore amazing and worthy of love.

Write a note to the struggling part of you, thanking yourself for the effort you've been putting in but letting yourself know that you can let go of the struggle and choose a lighter energy now. It's as simple as that—a firm decision and intention to change track.

Here are a few affirmations to signify this new direction:

- *From now on, I am choosing a lighter approach and energy for my Spanish journey.*
- *I am now open to allowing ease and flow into my Spanish learning.*
- *I am doing things differently now, with a focus on ease, fun, and lightness.*

Insert your affirmations in this note to yourself:

Dear Self,

Thank you for the effort you've been putting into learning Spanish so far. I'm here to let you know you can let go of the struggle and choose a lighter energy now.

- ♥ *From now on…*
- ♥ *I am…*
- ♥ *I choose…*
- ♥
- ♥

All my love,

Signed:
Date:

CHOOSE A SYMBOL TO REMIND YOU OF THIS SHIFT

A great way to cement this shift and keep your new intention, mindset, and energy at the forefront of your mind is to choose a symbol that will remind you to keep the energy light around your language learning practice. Get really quiet and still, and ask yourself what symbol you could choose to remind you to be more consistently present to this shift. Perhaps it's a heart, a crystal, a ray of sunshine, or a cloud. There are no wrong answers. It just has to feel right to you.

Practise bringing your symbol to mind at random moments during your day and feel into the new energy you're intending to bring into your language practice. You could post little visual reminders around your house, in your diary, or on bookmarks, wherever you'll see them often throughout your day. Each time your symbol comes to mind, take a moment to breathe in the intentions, energy, and feelings of your new, lighter, and more easeful approach to learning Spanish.

CAN YOU FALL IN LOVE WITH SPANISH A BIT MORE?

Here are a few questions to help you reignite the flame of Spanish joy within you.

What prompted you to want to study Spanish in the first place? Can you go back and see Spanish (the language, the people, the culture) with fresh eyes and a beginner's mind? Can you fall in love a little more with the incredible countries where Spanish is spoken? What are some of the things you love about Spain and Latin America? Can you be curious about the origin of Spanish words and start paying attention to interesting similarities you notice with English or other languages?

Write freely (and with as much emotion and detail as possible) about what comes up for you.

· *Heartful Spanish* ·

More space for heartstorming ways in which you can fall in love with Spanish a bit more:

BUSTING THROUGH BLOCK #8:
"I CAN'T UNDERSTAND SPANISH SPEAKERS. IT ALL GOES OVER MY HEAD!"

One of the things that holds us back from practising a foreign language is the feeling of being lost and "not understanding a thing" when we attempt to communicate with native speakers. They speak too fast for us, and they use words and expressions that are completely different from the language we learn in our Spanish classes and from textbooks. It can end up feeling a bit over our heads, so we stop even trying.

However, if we let those thoughts and feelings dominate our thinking, they'll grow in our subconscious mind, which will only feed the feelings of panic and fear, creating a vicious circle and making it increasingly difficult for us to understand or improve.

I've got two simple solutions for this problem, and they are both reiterations of what I've said before.

Firstly, it's completely normal to feel this way at times when learning languages, and we've all been there—seriously, everyone who ever learnt a language has been in this boat. But the only way is through, so I encourage you to recognise if this problem has been holding you back and then make a new commitment to getting exposure to native Spanish speakers in small, manageable chunks.

Secondly, once again, mindset is everything here. The key is to practise being OK with not understanding everything and to keep going with your listening/conversation/reading practice with a positive attitude. We're aiming for progress, not perfection. Just keep moving forward, and it'll get easier, I promise.

MAKE A NEW COMMITMENT TO ACCUSTOM YOUR EAR TO LISTENING IN SPANISH

Commit to doing some of the things we've covered before in bite-sized amounts: listening to podcasts or watching YouTube videos (slowed down a bit, if necessary), listening to the radio, or watching TV or films. Choose things you *want* to watch, so you're interested in understanding what's being said and you're curious to pick up the new vocab.

Conversation exchanges (see p.90) are another great way to improve your listening at the same time as your speaking skills.

What things are you going to commit to start doing more of, specifically to improve your listening practice?

CHANGE YOUR MINDSET TO BE MORE OK WITH DISCOMFORT AND OPEN TO GROWTH

It's important to notice any negative thoughts that keep cropping up. Things like these:

- *It's impossible to communicate with Spanish speakers.*
- *I don't understand a word they're saying.*
- *I panic whenever I hear a native speaker talking in Spanish at full speed.*
- *It's too fast for me and way over my head.*
- *I've given up listening to Spanish speakers because I just can't understand enough to get by.*

When you notice your inner critic coming up with these types of ruminations, thank it for the information, and then make sure you counteract the negative thoughts with some related positive affirmations that feel right to you.

You could try playing around with replacement thoughts like these:

- *I am practising listening to Spanish speakers in small, manageable chunks.*
- *I am OK with not understanding every single word. It feels good to push through and practise getting the gist.*
- *I am focusing on what I can understand, not what I can't.*
- *I am enjoying practising listening to Spanish in ways that feel doable and enjoyable for me, and I'm noticing how my ear is becoming more attuned now.*
- *I can listen to slowed-down Spanish, and my confidence is growing little by little.*
- *I love picking out new words that spark my curiosity when I listen to people speaking Spanish.*
- *I'm finding new ways to increase my exposure to Spanish listening, and it's starting to feel easier than before.*

How about turning your listening practice into a game? Instead of aiming for 100% comprehension at first, just pick out the bits you *can* understand and celebrate all wins, no matter how tiny.

My podcast, The Heartful Spanish Podcast, is designed to be a stepping stone on the way to listening to native Spanish speakers. The idea is that you listen either in bilingual version or in Spanish only followed by English only (or vice versa) to help you get more comfortable with not understanding everything at first, and to encourage you to learn to focus on the new words you hear that light up your joyful vocab radar.

Jot down any "ahas" from this section or write your favourite affirmations here:

More space to reflect on your ahas from this section or write affirmations that resonate for you:

READING IN SPANISH: PRACTICE FOR "JUST GETTING THE GIST" AND PUSHING ON THROUGH

If, like me, you love disappearing into a good book, reading in Spanish is a great way to boost your language exposure. You'll soak up the language, boost your vocab, and improve your grammar naturally by osmosis. And, most importantly, you'll gain the invaluable skill of "just getting the gist" and being OK with pushing on through when you don't understand everything.

It's ideal to read books or texts that are just slightly above your current level of Spanish, so you don't get bored or frustrated. There are plenty of articles and reading books for language learners that use simplified language and include vocabulary notes and comprehension exercises. I've suggested a few in the Resources for your Spanish section. These books have mixed reviews on Amazon though, so I encourage you to do your own research and choose books that appeal to you and your interests, ones that stretch your language skills just the right amount—enough to challenge you but not so much that you lose motivation.

Alternatively, you could try re-reading any book you've enjoyed in English (or another language) if you can find it in Spanish translation. In fact, if you can find your absolute all-time favourite book in Spanish, that's a fantastic way to keep motivated to push on through, "just getting the gist".

As part of my research for writing this workbook, I bought a book of short stories in Japanese by linguist Olly Richards (having already checked out his Spanish readers in my local bookshop). My Japanese used to be advanced level, but I have barely used it in the last 20 years or so (especially reading or writing), so I was unsure if intermediate level reading would be a bit over my head. I pushed on through anyway—reading in my hammock one lunchtime for the added enjoyment factor—and I managed to read the whole of the first chapter in my lunch break. It was only four pages long and not the most exciting of stories—and I could only understand about half of the words—but I pushed on through anyway and got enough of the gist to more or less follow what was going on. The sense of achievement afterwards was huge! Dear reader, I hope this inspires you to keep going when you're reading or listening to something that feels a little bit over your head.

BUSTING THROUGH BLOCK #9: "I CAN'T DO THIS!" OR "I'M NO GOOD AT LANGUAGES!"

I've added this block at the eleventh hour, inserting it into the final version of this workbook. I can't believe I overlooked this one in my earlier drafts, because it is *the* biggest mindset block when it comes to learning a language—or trying to succeed at (or just do) anything in life, actually.

This one comes up again and again for me in my life, not so often with languages, but definitely when it comes to things that involve learning new tech or attempting to do some boring admin task that I've been putting off.

"I'm no good at this" and "It's too difficult" tend to be my default setting for anything that feels hard or not in my "zone of genius". An implicit addendum to these thoughts is the silent conclusion "so I'm not even going to try".

I know logically that telling myself "I can't do this" is no way to find ease and flow (in whatever endeavour it is I'm attempting—or avoiding), but sadly, it's been a lifelong pattern for me to default to this type of thinking whenever things start feeling uncomfortable.

A timely example of this in my life is the seemingly ginormous (to me) challenge of "adding the finishing touches" to this very workbook. I've never edited my own writing before in such a big project, and it feels quite scary to put this out in the world, not to mention all the tech hurdles I still need to overcome, like how to format it for publication and how to sell it online.

Leo Babauta, the author of the Zen Habits blog, and his fabulous online community, the Fearless Living Academy, have been massively helpful for me in busting through these "It's too difficult, so I'm not going to try" patterns, motivating me to practise sitting with the uncertainty and the feelings of discomfort involved. Leo's work has been a big influence on me, and many of his "Uncertainty Challenge" exercises are echoed in this workbook.

Below are a few reflections and practices that are helping me change my "I can't" type thinking. I hope they help you if you're experiencing similar negative self-talk when it comes to your ability to learn Spanish.

SIT WITH THE DISCOMFORT

If this block of telling yourself "I can't do this" or "I'm no good at languages" sounds familiar to you, first, congratulate yourself for noticing the negative thought pattern. This is the crucial first step to modifying any habit. Change is on its way, my friend.

Next, spend a few moments sitting with the discomfort. Where do you notice it in your body? How does it feel? What words would you use to describe the bodily feelings that these thoughts produce in you? This doesn't have to take long. It can be just a minute or two of feeling the sensations and naming the emotions.

Then, take a few long, deep breaths and simply set the intention to be open to change.

It could be a simple shift in thoughts and feelings:

- → From "I can't" to "What if it were possible?"
- → From "I'm no good at this" to "I am open to improving my mindset and emotions around this"
- → From "I feel all this resistance to learning Spanish" to "I am ready to experience ease and flow in my Spanish"

Now, come back into your body and notice if it feels any different. Has there been a weight lifted from your shoulders? Does your heart area feel more expansive now? Do you feel a shift in your energy? Perhaps an openness that wasn't there before? Any shift, no matter how minor, is great. Celebrate it.

Finally, take action anyway, despite the discomfort you're feeling. A really tiny action is fine. Something you've been resisting that will make you feel good after doing it. You're taking your Spanish in a new direction now—the direction of ease and flow.

Repeat this simple exercise often, any time you notice yourself resisting your Spanish practice or thinking negative thoughts about your ability to improve. Every small win, when you sit with the difficult emotions *and proceed anyway*, is a step on the way to your big dreams. Keep on going, brave soul, one foot forward after another. Now, doesn't that feel better?

JUST START SOMEWHERE

Maybe the idea of reaching fluency feels like too big a goal for you right now. That's OK, my dear. Let's break it down into tiny chunks so you can just start somewhere. Because that's the only way to tackle a huge "impossible" goal.

Just choose one thing from all the suggestions you've read in this workbook so far (or from the Resources for your Spanish section) that appeals to you most. The one thing that feels like it's a doable step, it's fun, and it sparks joy or at least curiosity for you. Do it today, do a mini two-minute version of it, or schedule it in the diary for tomorrow. But don't skip it. And keep doing it, or versions of it, on a regular basis until your joyful Spanish practice becomes ingrained as a daily habit and you no longer need to force yourself to do it, because it finally feels enjoyable.

The great thing about "just starting somewhere" is that, by setting the bar really low, any small action you choose to take to practise your Spanish is a win. Repeated daily, your wins will start to create the feeling of "I can do this", "This is possible", and maybe even "This is fun/joyful!"

With time and consistency, your fluency dream will gradually start to feel less impossible and more inevitable. Baby steps, my friend. *Poquito a poco.*

PAIR IT WITH SOMETHING YOU LOVE

To take your focus away from "I can't" and towards "This is fun!", try pairing your Spanish practice with something you love, something that feels like a treat, something that you wouldn't often allow yourself to do on a regular basis.

For example, to try and bring back my former fluency in Portuguese, I've recently started a daily habit of reading in the language. To make it more feel-good and appealing to me, I've decided to pair it with sitting in my garden or hanging out in my hammock, two things that feel like a treat and that I'd love to do more of.

I've chosen the book *Maktub* by Paolo Coelho, which is a great choice because it's an easy read (whilst also being challenging enough to keep me learning), it's all about reflections on spiritual and psychological matters (things I love to read and think about), and it has short chapters, so I can easily read just a few pages at a time without losing the thread.

· Busting Through Your Blocks ·

How can you pair your Spanish practice with something you love that feels like a treat? Use this space to brainstorm your ideas.

OUR STORIES ARE NOT AN ACCURATE REFLECTION OF REALITY

The stories we tell ourselves really are just that—stories. Made-up limiting ideas in our heads that are often far from being a true reflection of reality.

Sipping a *tinto de verano* (see top tip below) on a rooftop terrace in Madrid a few years ago, my friend Raz shared some exciting news; she was moving to Barcelona in the autumn. But in the next breath, she confessed she was worried about the language barrier because she was living in Paris at the time and had struggled to reach fluency in French. She told me she had a bit of a thing about "not being good at languages". The thing is, Raz grew up trilingual in the UK, speaking Punjabi, Urdu, and English, so her confession blew my mind big time—a trilingual *chica* who thinks she's no good at languages?!

But I got it. And it stirred something deeply in me. I could totally see what was going on. As well as perhaps some underlying Eurocentric thinking regarding the value of French and Spanish compared with Urdu and Punjabi (aargh!), just look at the way she'd learnt the two groups—the Asian languages naturally by immersion and the European ones by sitting in a classroom learning verb tables. To me, it was a no-brainer. Raz had completely discounted her ability to speak Punjabi and Urdu as a skill because it was a normal and effortless part of her trilingual upbringing and environment, and therefore (to her mind), it didn't count as being "good at languages". (Nobody told her that's the way we're meant to learn languages.)

We often do this in life. We discount the things that come naturally to us as not being difficult to learn or as "nothing special" and certainly not worthy of praise. And, conversely, we see the things that don't come naturally to us as "difficult" and unusual or extraordinary, things that only gifted people can do or those lucky enough to have grown up in ideal circumstances. But these are all stories, illusions, distorted versions of reality, fabricated by the negativity bias in our brains and our very human tendency to be hard on ourselves.

> **Top tip:**
>
> Sip a *tinto de verano* and fall in love a little more with Spanish culture. A *tinto de verano* is a refreshing summery drink, a bit like sangria but with less alcohol. It's a simple mixture of red wine (*vino tinto*, hence the name) and lemonade or *gaseosa* (a lightly citrus-flavoured soda water). It's usually served over ice with a slice of lemon or orange—or both to make it extra citrusy (very high vibe). If you're staying off the booze, you can make an alcohol-free lookalike with red berry iced tea or grape juice in place of the *vino*. Make it for your loved ones at home, and don't forget to raise a glass to your new joyful path to fluency. ¡Salud!

THE STORIES WE TELL OURSELVES ARE INFLUENCED BY OUR CIRCUMSTANCES

OK, so you may have all these stories in your head about why you can't get fluent in Spanish. But hear me out here. This is important. There are many, many communities in this world, in countries like Luxembourg, South Africa, or India, where pretty much *everybody* speaks more than one language fluently. It's the norm. They grow up seeing everyone around them speaking two (or more) languages, so they don't have any of these preconceived ideas about it being difficult. In their daily lives, they *need* multiple languages to communicate and interact with others, and they learn them naturally through human connection, practice, and trial and error. In these bilingual and multilingual communities, nobody ever goes around telling themselves "I'm no good at languages" (at least not in relation to the local languages), because they *all* pick them up like a sponge.

Lucky them, I hear you say. Their circumstances are different. That's true, but the point is that with the right circumstances—when language practice is regular, natural, and enjoyable—*everyone* can do it. And that includes you, my dear.

So, if reaching fluency in Spanish feels like an impossible goal to you right now, all that's needed is a change in circumstances (i.e., environment, decisions, habits) to get you back on track. (The mindset shift will follow naturally if the circumstances are right.) And today, with all the amazing technology we have at our fingertips, it's easier than ever before to create opportunities to practise languages in a way that feels good, and to do it consistently and often.

We'll cover ways to do this in the next few sections: bringing in joy to your Spanish practice, creating a feel-good Spanish learning strategy and plan, and building consistency.

CHANGING OUR STORIES THE LONG WAY—THROUGH LIFE LESSONS

Like my friend Raz with her Punjabi and Urdu, I completely discounted my achievement of speaking five languages to fluency in my twenties because—thanks to the foreign language-friendly environment I grew up in—I knew that anyone can speak foreign languages, that it's easy and natural, and that absolutely everyone can do it given the right circumstances.

My unhelpful "story" was that I needed something else in order to be "useful", a skill other than languages, which are just a vehicle of communication after all. How very human that my brain chose to discount my language skills and focus instead on the fact that I was "not good enough" at anything "valuable". Thanks for that, negativity bias!

Paying too much heed to my stories has led me to a lifetime of trial and error, dabbling in different careers sometimes far removed from, and at other times more closely connected with, my love of languages. All that dabbling (and quite a few painful moments when I followed my head not my heart) helped me see that when you follow your heart in life, things have a habit of working out. And I'm sure you'll agree that's a much nicer story to focus on.

After a ton of spiritual and personal growth work, I now fully appreciate that my love of languages is part of my uniqueness and that the great joy I get from speaking different languages (and from sharing my language joy with others to help them see that speaking languages is not difficult or clever and that it's an ability we all have) is my raison d'être and maybe even my *ikigai*.

And, finally, I've realised that even my deep sensitivity and my story of being "not enough" have been a blessing too, because they've led me to accumulate a gazillion mindset tips and tricks and develop a love of psychology, all of which has enabled me to write this book for you now. Everything happens for a reason. I'm learning to trust in the meandering path and let my heart lead the way.

But that's the long way to change our stories. It's taken me a few decades or more (and *un montón de autoayuda*—a heap of self-help work) to get to this point. Wouldn't it be nice if there were a quicker, less tortuous route? Read on, my friend, because there is!

SOME TIPS ON CHANGING OUR STORIES THE QUICKER WAY

Psychologist and meditation teacher Tara Brach says that one of the most profound transformations that many people have when they meditate is the realisation that they don't have to believe their thoughts (Brach, 2014). She talks about how, with consistent meditation practice, a space opens up between how people think and how they react. This space enables us to make more conscious decisions from a broader perspective, based on our inner wisdom instead of on our old fear-based thought patterns.

By slowing down and setting a clear intention, we can simply drop the unhelpful thoughts and replace them with more helpful ones instead. It can all change on a dime.

Since my late twenties, a negative story I've been telling myself is that "it's hard to keep up five languages at once", so I've gradually let three of my languages go while I concentrated on "perfecting" my Spanish (a Sisyphean task if ever there was one!) and not losing my native English (talk about a fear-based worst-case scenario!).

Anyway, the world has changed a lot in the last twenty years, and I now know it's not hard to keep up five languages at the same time at all—*if you want it enough*. So, I'm changing that old story that's been holding me back for two decades.

And here's what's helping me:

1) Starting really small

    I allow myself to enjoy just one or two minutes a day of my other languages, so it feels really doable and easy.

2) Changing the environment
    I make it easy for myself by leaving out books in obvious places where I can just pick them up on my tea breaks throughout the day. (I drink a lot of tea, so this is a great trigger to remind me often.)

3) Making it enjoyable
    I choose things I love and/or enjoy—things that feel good and that I want to do because they're fun and because it feels like a treat to do them.

4) Upping my game gradually
   When I first decided to pick my rusty languages back up, I started off with just one or two minutes at a time, and now, a few months later, I'm up to five minutes. I do occasionally listen to a longer meditation or a whole podcast when I fancy it. This makes it a pleasure, not a chore.

5) Being kind to myself
   I'm not too strict about my language habits, and there are plenty of days when I forget to practise one or two of my rusty languages (or sometimes all three). And that's OK. I'm moving in the right direction, I'm doing better than I was before, and I'm focusing on my wins now, so it's all good.

6) Self-awareness
   When I notice myself slacking off with my good habits, I grab my journal and take some time to uncover the negative stories I've got playing in my head and the accompanying behaviours, and I brainstorm a few more helpful affirmations and practices instead.
   I find ways to pair the affirmations with habits I already have, like exercising or cleaning my teeth, and bingo, that's story changing the quicker way!

A SPACE TO REFLECT ON CHANGING YOUR STORIES

Can you see how your stories have been protecting you but also holding you back from becoming fluent? Can you get really still and observe the messages from your body wisdom and all the negative emotions associated with your stories, showing you this isn't the way forward?

We humans are *meant* to feel good. Our feelings are a compass, showing us what's good for us and what's not. Feeling stuck is a message (often a whole-body one) that something needs to change. Can you be open to a new, heart-led way of improving your Spanish?

Use the left-hand column to reflect on the stories you've been telling yourself in relation to your Spanish, and the right hand column for some new replacement stories that feel better to you and are more likely to lead you to improve your fluency.

Old stories	New stories
△ *I find it really hard to improve my Spanish, so I'm not going to even try.*	♥ *I am curious to try a new, light-hearted approach to improving my Spanish.*
△ *My Spanish has stagnated, and I am not motivated at all to practise.*	♥ *I am learning to see my Spanish practice in a new light, and I am ready to have fun with it.*
△ *I never seem to find the time to focus on improving my Spanish.*	♥ *I am finding fun and easy ways to fit my Spanish practice into my days.*

BRINGING IN THE JOY FACTOR

"Find a place inside where there's joy, and the joy will burn out the pain."
"Encuentra un lugar en tu interior donde haya alegría, y la alegría quemará el dolor."
~ Joseph Campbell, American writer and professor

· Bringing in the joy factor ·

JOYFUL ACTIVITIES BRAINSTORMING

Think about the things that bring you joy. Everyone has their own joyful activities, and yours will be unique to you. What would you do all day if money were no object? Ride horses, read poetry, write fiction, paint, travel, dance? What lights you up and makes you lose track of time? What subjects could you (and do you) talk about, read about, think about, and dream about till the cows come home?

Write freely below on the things that bring you joy. And if you're struggling to come up with ideas, it might help to go back to your childhood and recall the things you used to love doing before you got bogged down with adult obligations. Or perhaps you could brainstorm things you've always wanted to be good at but you've never tried your hand at or you don't do often enough.

The things that bring me joy are…

More space to journal on what brings you joy…

(Prompts recap: What would you do all day if money were no object? What lights you up and makes you lose track of time? What subjects could you—and do you—talk about, read about, think about, and dream about till the cows come home? Think back to your childhood and recall the things you used to love doing. What things have you always wanted to be good at but you've never tried or you don't do often enough?)

Bringing in the joy factor

BRAINSTORM NEW WAYS TO COMBINE YOUR JOYFUL ACTIVITIES WITH LEARNING SPANISH

Now it's time to link the things that bring you joy back to your Spanish learning. Use the box below to come up with ways you can do the things you identified in the previous exercise in Spanish (preferably in small doses—mini-immersions—at first).

Say, for example, you love watercolour painting. You could follow Latin American watercolour artists on Instagram, join a Spanish-speaking Facebook group for watercolour enthusiasts, take painting classes by Zoom with a teacher who's a native Spanish speaker, or watch YouTube videos in Spanish teaching you how to improve your painting technique.

Do this for as many as possible of the joyful activities that you listed in the previous exercise.

If one of your joyful activities is kundalini yoga, like me, you could follow Spanish kundalini teacher Naiara on Instagram at @nai_jainai and soak up the language as you enjoy her reels or her online classes. Or if, like Heartful Spanish podcast listener Sarah, you love embroidery, you could follow Mexican cross-stitcher Blanca @bordandoarte on YouTube to improve your technique and your language skills at the same time—double whammy! See the Resources section at the end of this workbook for more suggestions.

Joyful activity	Ways I could combine the activity with my Spanish practice

· Bringing in the joy factor ·

Some beautiful blank space for more notes…

This is the most important part of the workbook, so keep delving, have fun, and see what gems come up for you. Here's some more blank space for you to explore your heart's yearnings:

A WORD ON FINDING JOY IN IMMERSION

If you're a beginner or out of practice, you won't understand everything that native speakers say at first. That's how it's *supposed* to be with language immersion. It's like a "stretch goal". You just keep going as best you can and don't worry about 100% comprehension. The aim is to get comfortable with the discomfort. Treat each mini-immersion as a game: just see what you can pick up and—most importantly—enjoy the process.

The wonderful thing about linking your passions and interests with your language learning is that your love of the subject matter will magnify your desire to understand what's being said. You're also much more likely to get the gist because it's a subject that is close to your heart and you're familiar with what's being talked about. You'll soak up the language without even realising you're learning.

Now, you may be thinking, "I can't just dive in and listen to native speakers; it will be way over my head!" Fear not, my friend. It might take a little searching at first, but you will soon find people who speak clearly and simply, and you can start off with very short videos (e.g., Instagram reels or YouTube shorts), so it feels more doable.

The beauty of self-led language learning today is that the tech is on our side; you can slow down the play speed or use subtitles to help you understand more.

For complete beginners, at first you may want to just listen in Spanish and read the subtitles in English, seeing which words you can pick out. This needs to be done mindfully, with intention. If you find yourself ignoring the Spanish and just reading the English subtitles, it's time to take it up a notch.

When you feel ready for the challenge, or once your ear is more attuned, you can switch to Spanish subtitles, reading as you listen along, which will help your spelling, reading, and writing as well as your listening. Some complete beginners are happy to dive in at the deep end straight away, listening and reading in Spanish. The trick is to be OK with the discomfort and just treat it as a game, seeing which words you can understand and which new ones you learn.

 **Top tip**

There are two Chrome extensions called Language Reactor (previously Language Learning With Netflix) and Subtitles For Language Learning (Prime Video), which allow you to watch your favourite programs with subtitles and a dictionary function in Spanish, no matter what the original language is of the program you're watching. If this seems a bit too "hard core" language geeky for you, just try a few minutes at a time and only increase the time if it becomes a fun habit. Make sure you choose your favourite programs for the familiarity factor, so you're motivated to watch (and practise) often.

YOUR ENERGY AND YOUR "VIBES"

How in tune are you with your energetic levels and your "vibes"?[2] Think back to times in the past when you've felt energised, elated, or floating on air. What were you doing when you experienced these "high vibration" feelings? Where were you? What can you do now to bring similar feelings back?

---

[2] If the word "vibes" doesn't light your candle or sounds a bit too hippy for you, please don't be put off by the term; just think of vibes as feelings. And replace the words "high vibes" for "good feelings". We all have feelings. And they guide us towards our best life. Ignore them at your peril.

· Bringing in the joy factor ·

Some examples of activities that leave you feeling uplifted, energised, and "high vibe" might be doing exercise or sport, playing uplifting music, dancing around your kitchen, having a picnic with your loved ones, baking a cake or cookies, arranging flowers, or painting a picture.

Slowing down, making full use of all the senses, and paying attention to the present moment can all help elevate your vibrational state.

Write freely on what energises you and raises your vibes.

NOTICE YOUR VIBES AROUND LEARNING SPANISH

Now think about your current situation re Spanish and how you feel when you sit down to study (or when you think about "having" to improve your Spanish). How does that feel in your body?

Explore your feelings in the space below.

When I sit down to learn Spanish I feel...

Are the feelings you've identified very different from the feelings you described in the previous exercise? If so, I recommend you do one of the activities you've identified that boost your energy and make you feel "high vibe" *before* you sit down to study Spanish. Aim to do this every single time, and the difference in how you feel about your Spanish will be like night and day. A before and after on your Spanish-learning journey.

> 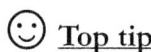 **Top tip**
>
> It's crucial to know when it's time to stop studying or practising Spanish too. It's far better to stop when you're on a roll and feeling good than to keep going until your head is ready to explode. If you stop while you're still enjoying it and having fun, you're more likely to want to pick it back up again without procrastinating next time. So again, a reminder: LAMFO, my friend. Little Amounts, Fun, and Often.

YOUR NEW FEEL-GOOD LEARNING STRATEGY

"It is our feelings that guide us and they can never lead us wrong."
"Son nuestros sentimientos los que nos guían, y nunca pueden llevarnos a error".

~ Jude Morgan, British author

WHAT IS A FEEL-GOOD LANGUAGE LEARNING STRATEGY?

Feel-good language learning needs to have these elements:

- **It must feel good to you**

When you think about your language practice, it should feel light, easy, and not so much of a stretch that you lose the enjoyment. Keep it "doable"—don't aim for big goals at first; just focus on learning a new word or two each time you sit down to learn. And get into the habit of congratulating yourself on your successes, no matter how small.

- **It must involve joy and fun**

The more you link your passions—the things that bring you joy—with your language learning, the easier and more enjoyable it will be for you to learn. Make joy and fun the essence of your language practice, and success will surely follow.

- **It needs to be consistent**

It's no use having one feel-good, joyful language session per month if that's the only time you pick up your Spanish in four weeks. For those who are just starting their journey to fluency or are aiming to make significant progress, the way to build consistency is to just keep showing up. Keep practising, five or six days a week, if possible, even if just in teeny tiny chunks. Try five minutes a day at first and build on that when it feels right to you. Little and often is the way to keep your language practice light and feeling good. Repeat after me: LAMFO, LAMFO, LAMFO forever!

- **It must spark your curiosity and eagerness to learn**

Make it a habit (or a game) to seek words and phrases that spark your "word joy" or make you sit up and note something interesting about them. Also, start to collect words and phrases that you think will come in handy. Nurturing an attitude of curiosity and eagerness to build up your word bank is essential for fast, "effortless" improvement.

- **You need to have a positive mindset**

Promise me you'll never sit down to learn Spanish when you're begrudging it and feeling like you "have to" do it. If you're feeling like this at the start of a session, take a moment to breathe and give yourself some self-compassion. Remind yourself of your "why", to uplift your intentions, and choose one of the practices in the SOS section below to bring yourself back to a more positive mindset, one that is more conducive to effortless learning.

- **You must have faith**

Believe in your ability to speak Spanish fluently. If you believe it can be done, that's half the battle, right there. I know you can do it. I hope you know it too. If you've struggled in the past, it's only because you may have been going about it the hard (not fun) way. Believe you can do it and believe it can be easy and fun (or at least be open to the possibility), and then watch the fluency flow in!

· Your new feel-good learning strategy ·

BRAINSTORM IDEAS FOR YOUR NEW FEEL-GOOD LEARNING PLAN

Now it's time to come up with a new plan that reflects your new feel-good learning strategy. What is a realistic amount of time you can dedicate to your language learning? What self-learning activities are you going to commit to? Make sure you start small and choose things that feel good to you. (See your answers from the Brainstorm New Ways to Combine your Joyful Activities with Learning Spanish activity on page 133.)

Use the space below to reflect on these prompts.

YOUR NEW FEEL-GOOD SPANISH LEARNING PLAN

Commitment and contract:

🕐 I commit to spending _____ minutes per day, _____ days a week, on feel-good Spanish learning.

☺ My vision for my Spanish is _____
_____

🔥 I intend to feel _____
_____

💻 📖 I will use the following platforms/genres/methods/books/series:
_____
_____
_____
_____, which

feel fun and light to me.

✏ I will track my progress each week by _____
_____

🎉 And I will celebrate my wins by _____
_____

✓ For accountability, I will check in _____
_____ (how/where) every _____ (how often) at _____ (when/time).

· *Your new feel-good learning strategy* ·

🆘 If I veer off course, I will do the following things: _____

_____

_____

_____

_____

💡 Some other things I want to remember: _____

_____

_____

Signed: _____

Date: _____

A NOTE ON KEEPING IT "FEEL-GOOD"

Set the bar low and keep raising it gradually. If you're feeling resistant to getting started, just aim for five minutes of Instagram or YouTube in Spanish a day at first (or even two minutes if that's too much). Set the bar so ridiculously low you cannot fail. And make sure you reward yourself when you reach your target for the day or week. This will reinforce the feel-good factor and strengthen the habit even more.

BUILDING CONSISTENCY

"Just trying to do something—just being there, showing up—is how we get braver. Self-esteem is about doing."

"Simplemente tratar de hacer algo, simplemente estar allí, aparecer, es cómo nos volvemos más valientes. La autoestima se trata de hacer."

~ Joy Browne, American psychologist and TV presenter

Consistent practice is key in language learning. The next few exercises will help you build consistency and stick to your plan: track your progress, find an accountability buddy or group, and notice how far you've come.

TRACK YOUR PROGRESS

A habit tracker is a great tool to ensure you keep up your daily Spanish practice. There are plenty of apps that are great for this. Some examples of habit-tracking apps that come highly recommended are Habitica, Beeminder, and Habitshare.

If you don't want to use screens, you could simply print out a monthly or weekly habit tracking chart and stick it on your fridge door or wall, somewhere you'll see it every day. There are a couple of simple PDF habit trackers on my website, www.heartfulspanish.com, for you to download and print out.

Consistency is everything, so choose your high-vibe language habits carefully and commit to them for 30 days. According to a study by researchers at University College London, it can take between 18 and 254 days to build a habit, and on average 66 days (Lally et al., 2009). I recommend you take it one month at a time, which will help keep it feeling doable, and you will soon notice improvements.

FIND AN ACCOUNTABILITY BUDDY OR GROUP

Having an accountability buddy will really help you stay motivated to keep up your Spanish practice. This can be a friend or family member, or someone you've met online who's also working on their habits, whether related to Spanish practice or any other goal. (You could try posting in the Heartful Spanish Facebook group to find an accountability partner with similar needs in terms of frequency and contact.)

Share your goals with your buddy or group, and then agree on how often you're going to check in with each other and how you'll be communicating (e.g., instant messaging, via a shared Google Doc, or similar). You could do check-ins every week (or even every day, say, five days a week, if you feel you want that level of accountability) to make sure you both stay on track. Additionally, monthly or bi-monthly chats would be helpful, to discuss any issues that come up and brainstorm ways to overcome them. The aim is to keep your language practice feeling joyful, light, and feel-good.

Another fabulous accountability tool is Focusmate. It's a platform that connects you, via video call, to other people who want to focus on their goals, distraction free. This has been a total lifesaver for me as a freelancer. It helps me use my time well and stick to what I say I'm going to do. (I'm in a session right now as I write this!)

NOTICE HOW FAR YOU'VE COME

Research tells us that optimism is a predictor of success, both in life and in learning (see Mishra, 2012; Rand, 2020). One of the key habits of optimistic people is that they regularly take the time to celebrate their wins and congratulate themselves on their progress, even when things aren't going quite as well as they'd hoped. Applying this to our language learning, if we can adopt the habit of regularly pausing to notice how far we've come and to celebrate our wins, it will be a game changer in shifting the energy from stagnancy to flow.

Can you remember when you knew no Spanish at all? Can you take stock for a moment of how many things you know how to say now? Recognise that you've made progress, even if not as much as you'd like. Cut yourself some slack. Beating yourself up never helped anyone, so stop that right now, please. Find a win—any little win—on your Spanish learning journey and *celebrate*.

And this is why we have a habit tracker and the joyful vocab notebook—so we can take stock of the tiny wins on our learning journey that would otherwise go unnoticed. Make it a habit, perhaps once a week or more often if you like, to stop and notice your progress. If you find you've not done as much as you'd have liked to on a given week, there's always something you can celebrate—even if it's just noticing that you've fallen off the wagon. It's all good. Language learning is rarely a straight line to fluency. It's more of a learning curve and not always a smooth one, more like a generally upwards zig-zag or a journey of ups and downs. Celebrate that you're doing this. You're amazing.

SOME SOS TOOLS AND TIPS

"We may encounter many defeats but we must not be defeated."

"Podemos encontrar muchas derrotas, pero no debemos ser derrotados."

~ Maya Angelou

· Some SOS tools and tips ·

Here are a number of SOS tips and tricks for if (or rather, when!) you veer off track and get out of the habit of regular feel-good Spanish practice.

SELF-COMPASSION AND ACCEPTANCE

Be kind to yourself, my friend. We all slip up from time to time. It's called being human.

Here's what to do:

1. Congratulate yourself for noticing that your feel-good Spanish practice has fallen by the wayside, because that's the first step in getting back on track.

2. Acknowledge that you, like many others, have got temporarily side-tracked from your joyful language habits, and realise that it's just a case of ebb and flow—part and parcel of being human.

3. Give yourself a bit of love. Put a hand on your heart and breathe. Say, "It's OK, my love. It happens to all of us at times. It's no big deal. You can start anew any time that feels right."

4. Resolve firmly to pick your Spanish practice back up, but this time in a very gentle way that feels doable to you. (If that means just learning one word or phrase per day, then that's what you do.)

5. Seek some accountability and start tracking your daily practice (in one of the ways we discussed in the Track your Progress section). You've got this.

If you feel called to deepen your self-compassion practice, Dr Kristin Neff, one of the world's leading psychologists in this field, has a ton of excellent resources and free audios for download on her website, www.self-compassion.org.

Clinical psychologist and meditation teacher Dr Tara Brach also offers many wise and insightful talks, meditations, and courses on the subjects of radical acceptance and compassion (for self and others). See Dr Tara's website at www.tarabrach.com.

AFFIRMATIONS FOR A RESET

Here are a few simple affirmations for when it's all gone to pot and you need to reset.

- ♥ *I choose to give myself self-compassion for my Spanish journey so far, and from now on I intend to keep it light, fun, and feeling good.*
- ♥ *I am ready to pick up my Spanish again, with a newfound resolve to focus on feel-good learning and taking the relaxed, joyful route to fluency.*
- ♥ *I am getting back on track with my Spanish.*
- ♥ *I am starting again today, and I am finding new ways to boost my Spanish that feel right to me.*
- ♥ *I am taking tiny steps to improve my Spanish, and I am focusing on small wins every day. It all adds up, and I am on my way to finding fluency with ease and joy.*
- ♥ *I am always guided. The answers are always within.* (This is a wonderful affirmation for life and language learning. I use it all the time to bring me back to centre.)

SET A NEW TINY GOAL AND COMMIT TO IT

Right here, right now, set yourself a goal that's so easy you can't possibly miss it: one new word or two minutes of practice per day.

And pinky-promise (yourself or a friend) you will stick to it. Simple solutions are the best.

IF YOU'VE BURNT OUT, TAKE A BREAK

If you've been working hard at your Spanish but feeling like you're spinning your wheels and not making much progress, consider taking a break. Come back afresh in a few days' time, armed with a firm resolve and the exercises in this workbook to help you lead yourself to fluency via a completely different, fun, and feel-good route.

Let this break be like a line in the sand: a before and after in your approach to fluency. No more being hard on yourself. It's time to choose the easier path. Self-compassion and heart-guided action will be your new default from now on.

EFT TAPPING

Have you ever tried EFT tapping? It stands for emotional freedom technique, and it may look weird, but it's surprisingly effective for solving all sorts of emotion-based problems, and there's increasing evidence to support its efficacy in the scientific studies (see Clond, 2016; Nelms & Bruce, 2016, Stapleton et al., 2022). It's also very simple and easy to do in a short amount of time.

EFT involves tapping on a number of meridian points around the body whilst saying different statements about your feelings to acknowledge (and then relieve) the stress or anxiety you feel about the issue.

You can easily learn the basic method on YouTube by searching for videos using the words "EFT tapping explanation for beginners". Brad Yates has a good one called "Intro to EFT". The Tapping Solution's Jessica Ortner also has a great explanation for beginners called "Tapping 101", available on the website www.thetappingsolution.com. And the Tapping Solution app has an audio called "Intro to tapping (Start here)" that you can access if you download the free version of the app.

Once you are familiar with how tapping works, you can use it to tap on the mindset issues and blocks you identified in the earlier exercises. EFT is great because, unlike "toxic positivity" or switching automatically straight to fake optimism, it allows you to acknowledge the difficult feelings you are experiencing, "feel all the feels", and then let them go.

A TAPPING OVERVIEW FOR BEGINNERS

First, you define the issue you're going to tap on (e.g., *I feel embarrassed to speak Spanish because I feel like I should speak better by now*) and rate the discomfort that it causes you on a scale of one to ten.

Next, you say a set-up statement, which outlines the problem and then adds an element of self-acceptance, while tapping on the side of the hand (the karate chop point). The set-up statement is usually repeated three times, acknowledging the feelings associated with the issue and expressing self-acceptance. (Example: *Even though I feel embarrassed by my Spanish at times, I love and accept myself exactly as I am.*)

After that, you do a round or two of tapping on the problem, going around each of the other tapping points on the body in turn with around five to seven gentle taps at each point, expressing the feelings you have regarding the issue at hand. (Example: *It feels so frustrating and embarrassing not to speak better Spanish than I do. / I feel so stuck and limited by my lack of ability to communicate in Spanish. / I can feel all this frustration and embarrassment in my body.*)

Finally, you do another round or two of tapping on the solution, whereby you affirm that you are open to experiencing new feelings (such as feeling more confident, more comfortable, or happier when you speak Spanish). (Example: *I can start to believe in my abilities now. / I am open to feeling joy in my Spanish. / I am open to finding ease and flow.*)

After the tapping, check back in with your feelings and revisit your rating from one to ten. Has some of the difficult emotion surrounding your issue dissipated or lightened? Are you feeling any better than when you started this exercise? If you feel the need, you can go back and do more rounds of tapping, to release more of the unwanted emotions surrounding your situation.

THE TAPPING POINTS

For more information or greater clarity on the EFT tapping points, a simple internet search will bring up plenty of images showing the EFT tapping points, but here I will outline the main points you will tap on. When we say "a round of tapping", it means going once around all of these points, moving from one point to another with the natural break in the sentences (e.g., the end of a sentence, or a line in the next exercise).

- Eyebrow
- Side of eye
- Under eye
- Under nose
- Chin
- Collarbone
- Under arm
- Top of head

AN EXAMPLE OF AN EFT TAPPING SESSION FOR FEELING EMBARRASSED TO SPEAK SPANISH

Here is an example of an EFT tapping session to address the issue of feeling embarrassed to speak Spanish. It will work best for you if you change the wording to adapt it to your specific circumstances and feelings.

Set-up statement (repeat three times)

Karate chop point: *Even though I am embarrassed to speak Spanish because I feel I should speak better by now, I love and accept myself exactly as I am.*

A round or two of tapping on the problem

Eyebrow: *I feel so embarrassed.*

Side of eye: *It feels so frustrating and embarrassing to not speak better Spanish than I do.*

Under eye: *I feel so stuck and limited by my lack of ability to communicate in Spanish.*

Under nose: *All this frustration, all this embarrassment,*

Chin: *I can feel it in my body.*

Collarbone: *And it doesn't feel good.*

Under arm: *I realise I've been holding myself back*

Top of head: *And beating myself up.*

Eyebrow: *These feelings of embarrassment and frustration are not helping me progress.*

Side of eye: *I want to stop feeling these feelings.*

Under eye: *They are keeping me from reaching my fullest potential.*

Under nose:	*Sometimes I feel this stuckness and embarrassment, even when I'm not speaking Spanish.*
Chin:	*Just the thought of speaking Spanish can start these feelings of frustration off again.*
Collarbone:	*It feels constricted in my body.*
Under arm:	*It's OK to feel and notice these feelings.*

A few rounds of tapping on changing our mindset and becoming open to the solution or the ideal outcome:

Top of head:	*But what if I could see these feelings of frustration as a helpful sign letting me know I need to change track?*
Eyebrow:	*What if I could let go of these feelings and start to feel better about my Spanish?*
Side of eye:	*Wouldn't it be nice if I could stop focusing on how embarrassing it is to speak Spanish…*
Under eye:	*…And just enjoy the process of communicating and learning?*
Under nose:	*Perhaps I could focus on enjoying the heart-to-heart connection of communicating with another human being,*
Chin:	*And being understood and making breakthroughs despite my imperfect Spanish.*
Collarbone:	*I can start to focus on the tiny moments when I don't feel so embarrassed,*
Under arm:	*When I experience breakthroughs and small successes with my Spanish.*
Top of head:	*It feels so good to be able to communicate and get the message across.*

Eyebrow:	*It feels so liberating to let go of all the "shoulding" on myself...*
Side of eye:	*...that has caused me frustration and embarrassment in the past.*
Under eye:	*I can feel it in my body.*
Under nose:	*And it's a huge weight off.*
Chin:	*I can let go of all the frustration.*
Collarbone:	*I can let go of the need to be perfect.*
Under arm:	*It's safe to let go of these old beliefs now.*
Top of head:	*And replace them with thoughts and feelings that help me relax about my Spanish.*
Eyebrow:	*And empower me to enjoy the learning process.*
Side of eye:	*I am open to feeling a shift.*
Under eye:	*It's safe for me to imagine wonderful outcomes for my Spanish now.*
Under nose:	*I can believe in my abilities now.*
Chin:	*I am stepping into my fullest potential*
Collarbone:	*And I am doing things differently now.*
Under arm:	*I am open to feeling joy in my Spanish.*
Top of head:	*I am open to finding ease and flow.*

Disclaimer

I've been using EFT for a few years now. I've read a few books on the subject and done plenty of tapping with practitioners, but I'm not an EFT expert. If you would like to explore this further and see how EFT can help you improve your language learning mindset and abilities, I highly recommend you work 1:1 with a reputable EFT practitioner.

RESOURCES: MINDSET, JOY, & SUCCESS

"What really counts isn't whether your instrument is Baroque or modern; it's your mindset."

"Lo que realmente cuenta no es si tu instrumento es barroco o moderno; es tu forma de pensar."

~ Simon Rattle, orchestra conductor

Over the last eight months or so, as I've been writing this little workbook, I've become more and more astounded at how all the mindset tips and tricks that have helped me live a happier, more fulfilled life are also highly applicable to language learning. I can't count the number of times I've said in this workbook, "And as in life, so in language learning!"

I hope you'll see for yourself how these practical resources can help you live your full potential—both in life itself and in your experience of learning and improving your Spanish.

BOOKS

Emotional Intelligence by Daniel Goleman

I first read *Emotional Intelligence* by Daniel Goleman when I was in my twenties, and I immediately loved it. Being highly sensitive and having a tendency toward introversion, I had often felt slightly out of place in lots of life situations, and this book highlighted to me, for the first time, that I wasn't "less than" less sensitive people after all and that I actually had a bit of a superpower: my deep empathy. Reading this book opened my eyes to the fact that emotional awareness is key to thriving in life. And I now know with all my heart that this awareness is essential to successful language learning too, especially in those situations when it doesn't come naturally at first.

The Tapping Solution: A Revolutionary System for Stress-Free Living by Nick Ortner

If you're interested in learning more about EFT tapping, I recommend Nick Ortner's book *The Tapping Solution: A Revolutionary System for Stress-Free Living*, which makes a compelling case for the efficacy of tapping. When I was reading this book I started using the Tapping Solution App on a daily basis. Without both of these fabulous resources, I'm not sure I'd have got through the very strict national lockdown we had in Spain in 2020 with my sanity intact!

EFT is *such* a powerful tool for changing limiting beliefs; it's only natural that it would also be effective in helping people to believe in their abilities to speak and understand foreign languages.

Creative Visualization by Shakti Gawain

When I read Shakti Gawain's wonderful book, *Creative Visualization,* and started to incorporate more relaxation and visualisation into my days, I was gobsmacked at the amazing shifts and manifestations that started to appear in my life.

Truth be told, I did most of the exercises quite half-heartedly at the time, so I can only imagine what would happen if I did them with more gusto (perhaps with a friend or a group for accountability). The one that did stick with me for life was the pink bubble technique. Try it for your Spanish fluency dream and see if it works for you.

Ask and It Is Given by Abraham Hicks

Now, this one is a little "out there", so don't say I didn't warn you! I would never have picked up this book if it hadn't been highly recommended to me by someone I respect and admire. And I'm so glad I did, because it's full of fabulous practices that have helped me "magically" create a better life for myself in so many ways. A great one to dip into when you're feeling stuck in any area or struggling with difficult emotions, or even if you're already feeling good but would love to boost your levels of joy and ease even more.

My favourite takeaway from this book is a powerful exercise called "segment intending". This is where you pause to set a clear intention at the beginning of each "segment" in your day (e.g., changing to a new activity or even just moving to a new room in the house), focusing on the outcome you want and how you want to feel. Segment intending helps me to be more present in my life, and to keep coming back to my priorities over and over again throughout the day.

Positive Energy by **Dr Judith Orloff**

I've been reading this book, *Positive Energy,* by psychiatrist Dr Judith Orloff on and off for a couple of years now. I still haven't got to the end because I find that after I finish each chapter, I need to take a break and let it all sink in. It has tons of fabulous exercises and illustrative examples to help you improve your energy levels and tune into the energy around you.

My main takeaway so far is that when we rush through life without full awareness of our energy and the things that affect it, we miss out on so much and fail to even scratch the surface of our fullest potential in health, wellbeing, relationships, learning, and more.

Trust Your Vibes by **Sonia Choquette**

This was a quick read (and, again, quite "out there"!), but it left a lasting impression on me. We are born deeply intuitive, but society and our education system tend to kill it, little by little, over the years. This light-hearted read helped me start to get it back.

Our intuition is always available to guide us, if only we'll slow down and listen to it. Trust your intuition on your Spanish-learning journey, and follow the things you are called to do.

A great intuition-building practice is to journal daily on questions such as, "What do I most need to know (or do) to improve my Spanish?" as well as questions related to other areas of life, such as, "What do I most need to do to improve my mood/health/career/relationship?" The answers always come when you get still and listen.

The Complete Works of Florence Scovel Shinn: The Game of Life and How to Play It; Your Word Is Your Wand; The Secret Door to Success; and The Power of the Spoken Word

It is one of my guilty pleasures to pick up early 20th-century classics of positive thought and self-help. They are classics for a reason. I devoured this four-in-one gem of a book with great delight when I came upon it. It's an easy, uplifting read, and it contains a lot of wisdom (including quotes from the Bible) that will help anyone who is open to a spiritual approach make changes in their life.

If Bible quotes are not your thing, you can just skim over them, as I used to do with the next book, when I read it during my twenties and thirties phase of rejecting my Catholic upbringing and all Christianity-associated language. You can gain a lot from the wisdom in the words if you keep an open mind. These days, I'm much more open to learning from all the religions, just as long as no one's shoving it down my throat and telling me it's "the only way".

The Power of Your Subconscious Mind by **Dr Joseph Murphy**

Belonging to the same genre as the previous title, this book was the first of its kind to come into my life. I picked it up in a tiny second-hand book shop nearly thirty years ago, and it's been on my bedside table ever since. Each chapter has a list of bullet points summarising the main ideas, and these are fabulous for a quick "once-over" at bedtime to cement them into my subconscious. Reading this book initiated my lifelong love of positive affirmations. (A true salve for the previous default self-criticism and self-doubt that often tended to dominate my thoughts as a sensitive child and young adult.)

Change Your Thoughts, Change Your Life and *There's a Spiritual Solution to Every Problem* by Dr Wayne Dyer

Psychologist and author Dr Wayne Dyer had a wonderful ability to draw from ancient texts from all of the religions, sharing insights and wisdom that can be applied to everyday life to help us live with more ease and clarity and create the lives of our dreams. I love all his books, but these two titles stand out as firm favourites.

Being Supernatural by Dr Joe Dispenza

This book explains how we can change our thoughts and emotions to transcend the limitations of our past and break the habit of living in addictive patterns of stress and negativity. Through meditation and living in the present instead of dwelling on the past, we can improve our lives in all areas—mood, relationships, finances, and health.

If we tap into an elevated emotion—such as joy, appreciation, or love—when we meditate, we can fire ourselves up and rewire our brains to create new habits and experience higher states of consciousness. It's all about becoming the person we want to be, first in the imagination, and then watching that vision come to fruition in our lives.

Atomic Habits by James Clear

The main message of *Atomic Habits* by James Clear is that if we can look at the habit changes we want to introduce and create miniscule versions of those habits, they will be easier for us to implement and stick to. Practising our tiny habits may not seem like much on any given day, but over time they add up to huge changes.

Another helpful takeaway is that we can make it easy for ourselves to practise our habits by "stacking" them (i.e., pairing them with other habits we already do). For example, when I clean my teeth every morning and every night, I can say my affirmations while looking in the mirror. Or, when I make my bed in the morning, I can leave a book on my pillow to ensure I remember to read at bedtime.

Similar to the teachings of Dr Joe Dispenza, but viewed from a less esoteric, more practical perspective, James Clear also discusses the idea of habit change through identity change. Instead of setting goals that you want to achieve, Clear encourages you to *set a vision for the person you want to become* and then practise the habits that that ideal person would practise.

So, to become the type of person who is fluent in Spanish (i.e., a person who experiences ease and flow when they speak, listen to, read, and write the language), start dedicating some time every day to experiencing ease and flow in your Spanish practice in a way that feels right for you. Your tiny, easeful, fun Spanish habits are the way you prove to yourself, one day at a time, that you are becoming the person you envisaged.

Peace Is Every Step: The Path of Mindfulness in Everyday Life by Thich Nhat Hanh

I read the gentle teachings of Thich Nhat Hanh when my boys were little, and his words touched my heart (and mind) deeply. I'm still a work in progress, but this book and many of his other titles have helped me to start to remedy the lifelong tendency I've had of rushing through my days, whizzing from one task to the next, without appreciating the beauty of the "here and now" right in front of me.

When we slow right down and experience more peace, we are able to live more intentionally and more in alignment with the person we want to be. Bringing peace into our every step is such a simple, portable reminder to be more aware of the miracles of life and thus to live more in the present, prioritising what's important to us, moment to moment.

The Magic by Rhonda Byrne

This is another book that I simply wouldn't have picked up if it hadn't been highly recommended by someone I respect and trust. But it has left me truly gobsmacked, on more than one occasion, at how miraculous the exercises have been in improving my relationships and life circumstances. Give it a try—but get a buddy to do it with you for accountability to keep you going.

PODCASTS

Feel Better, Live More **by Dr Rangan Chatterjee**

I love Dr Rangan Chatterjee's four-pronged approach to living a happier, healthier life. The four areas he focuses on are sleep, exercise, relaxation, and food. I'm a firm believer that when we take steps to help ourselves feel better and live a healthier life, we are able to show up in the world as our best selves more consistently. It's all about making better decisions, moment to moment, and getting clear on our priorities as to what's important.

My favourite episodes were the interviews with Dr Joe Dispenza and Dr Tara Swart, two experts who talk about the science behind the law of attraction, albeit from very different perspectives. I also loved the interviews with Jay Shetty on happiness, manifesting, purpose, and passion.

All of these areas of wisdom can be massively helpful in creating the life of your dreams, including, of course, your dream of reaching fluency in Spanish.

School of Greatness **by Lewis Howes**

Former all-American athlete Lewis Howes interviews extremely successful individuals, on a broad range of subjects—spirituality, mindset, relationships, entrepreneurship, law of attraction, and more. Lewis is such a great interviewer and an all-round lovely human, and I could binge listen to his show (or watch it—it's also on YouTube) till the cows come home.

YOUTUBE

Creative Visualisation

Check out Lilou Macé's channel for a variety of videos on creative visualisation. I've been using these for years, especially the ones called "Dream job", "Quick and effective visualisation", and "Multiple bubbles" (this last one for when I've got three things I want solved or dreams I want to come to fruition).

www.youtube.com/user/liloumace

The Silva Method

Another technique, very similar to creative visualisation, is the Silva Method. There's a fantastic (and free!) Mindvalley webinar on the subject.

www.mindvalley.com

Here's the Silva method's 20-minute guided centring exercise, read by Vishen Lakhiani of Mindvalley.

www.youtube.com/watch?v=h_4GDXWBPCk

And here's a short (9 minute) Silva method visualisation on YouTube, led by Indian actress Raageshwari Loomba.

www.youtube.com/watch?v=b3OKJTd1ZSg

Tap With Brad

The wonderful EFT tapping expert Brad Yates has a tapping video for just about everything under the sun. Actually, I've just looked, and he doesn't have a video specifically for language learning, but some others that might be helpful include "Speaking clearly", "Enhancing brain function", and "Focus on desired results". Check them out and see if they help you in relation to your Spanish. If you're new to tapping, check out Brad's video "Intro to EFT" first.

WEBSITES

Dr Kristen Neff www.self-compassion.org

Research psychologist Dr Kristen Neff is one of the world's leading experts on self-compassion. Her website has tons of information on the research in this area as well as meditations, courses, and exercises you can do to learn this hugely life-enhancing practice.

This quote from Dr Neff's website resonates deeply with me: "You may try to change in ways that allow you to be more healthy and happy, but this is done because you care about yourself, not because you are worthless or unacceptable as you are." This pretty much describes in a nutshell the gradual process I've been on (and am still on) of self-transformation from "self-help junkie" to "self-compassionate human who dreams of shining her unique light and helping others shine theirs".

Tara Brach www.tarabrach.com

The wise and gentle teachings of psychologist and meditation teacher Tara Brach have helped me immensely. Her website has tons of excellent resources (meditations, talks, courses) for learning about self-acceptance, self-compassion, happiness, loving kindness, self-realisation, and other related topics. Highly recommend.

My Project Me with Kelly Pietrangeli www.myprojectme.com

I'm so glad I came across Kelly's blog *Project Me For Busy Mothers* some ten years ago when I was "struggling with the juggling" of being a working mum with little kids. With Kelly's gentle guidance, I've been able to create a much healthier work-life balance for myself and live happier in most of the life areas, most of the time.

Positive Psychology Ikigai Tests

www.positivepsychology.com/ikigai-test-questionnaires/

I went through a tough period in my mid-twenties, feeling lost and directionless, and the subject of *ikigai* and life purpose have been a bit of an obsession for me ever since, together with a heightened need for things that bring me joy. It's been a *very* meandering path so far, but I'm loving the journey, and I feel like I'm getting closer to my *ikigai* and to my joy, even with the writing of this book.

If you feel a similar curiosity towards finding your *ikigai*, this is a great website with a few questionnaires and thought-provoking questions that may help you narrow it down. The world needs us all to come alive to our unique joy and share it with the people around us (in big and little ways).

Focusmate www.focusmate.com

What can I say about this wonderful virtual coworking platform? I love it so much. Focusmate has a calendar-style booking system that pairs you with someone, anywhere in the world, who wants to focus at the same time as you. You can choose between sessions of 25, 50, or 75 minutes at practically any hour of the day.

It's amazingly effective at getting you to do the things you're procrastinating on and to be more conscious of your time use. It's also fun for "meeting" people all over the world who are working on a huge diversity of projects—whether decluttering their junk, getting their taxes done, doing their morning or evening routine, or just getting on with their daily work.

This little workbook would not exist without Focusmate. I am eternally grateful.

Nirvana www.nirvanahq.com

Nirvana is a fantastic productivity and organisation website and app that helps me to keep all my to-dos in one manageable place. I wouldn't be without it.

Trello www.trello.com

Trello is another great website and app for organising your to-do list. I used to use Trello to keep track of all my projects, but the sheer volume of "brainstormed-but-never-looked-at" ideas I kept there got so unwieldy that I decided to start all over again with Nirvana.

The Tapping Solution www.thetappingsolution.com

Here's the website where you will find the wonderful work of the Ortner siblings, Jessica, Nick, and Alex, of The Tapping Solution. See their "Tapping 101" for the basic introduction to EFT tapping.

APPS

Insight Timer www.insighttimer.com

Insight Timer is my go-to meditation app. It has meditations and courses on every subject you could possibly think of, as well as music for relaxation, meditation, and spirituality. There are an increasing number of Spanish-speaking teachers on Insight Timer too, which would make it a great way to combine spirituality and Spanish practice, if that feels right to you.

The Tapping Solution App www.thetappingsolution.com

The Tapping Solution app helped me get through those initial few months of the pandemic and the extremely strict lockdown we experienced here in Spain. I have since downgraded to the free version, which I use occasionally for pain relief or when I can't sleep. Both versions of the app are excellent.

Habit apps

I haven't found the perfect habit app for me yet, but I know many people swear by Habitica, an app based on gaming that is very popular—and free to use. Other habit apps that come highly recommended include Beeminder and Habitshare.

I'm currently using SnapHabit, which I like because it's nice and simple. It allows sharing with friends for extra accountability, but I haven't worked out how to optimise the notifications, so I sometimes fall off the "good habits" wagon without even realising it. I'd love to hear from you if you find a habit-building app you love.

COURSES

The High Vibe Journey by Kelly Pietrangeli

Kelly Pietrangeli's "High Vibe Journey" is a four-week course on spiritual and personal growth that has had a profoundly transformational effect on my life, helping me to cement all the years (decades) of self-help into lasting changes, enabling me to live with more ease and joy as well as massively improved relationships with my loved ones and those around me. Kelly also offers follow-up courses that are equally life-changing. See Kelly's website for details. www.myprojectme.com

Living Life from the Heart by Rachel Hillary

I found this 10-day course by Rachel Hillary on the Insight Timer meditation app, and it moved me deeply at exactly the time I needed it. I recommend this beautiful course for anyone who is curious to learn more about living more in tune with the energy of the heart. Here's the Insight Timer website for more info.

www.insighttimer.com/rachelhillary/courses

COMMUNITIES

I am a member of various online communities of wonderful human beings, most of whom I've never met in real life. The connections and support I have found have helped me immensely in taking the leap and writing this workbook.

Soul Explorers (formerly Project We)

I know you've read the name Kelly Pietrangeli a lot already in this workbook, but when something changes my life for the better, I can't help but shout it from the rooftops! In Kelly's wonderful Soul Explorers community, I have found a fabulous group of like-hearted women. We inspire each other and raise each other up to live our best lives and show up as our best selves in the world. Join us?

www.myprojectme.com

IWBB (International Women Building Businesses)

This fantastic community of women in business—led by Natasha Kennedy, Clodagh Beaty, and Candy Lee LaBalle—has helped me tremendously in the process of making the leap from passion project to online business. I've loved the coworking sessions with my fellow Vaultini *chicas*, and the online group sessions and networking brunches in Madrid have been heaps of fun, inspiring me to step up and shine my light (and grow my business too—on it, Natasha! ¡*Mil gracias!*) To find out more, go to

www.facebook.com/groups/iwbbabroad.

Fearless Living Academy

Leo Babauta's Fearless Living Academy (FLA), and within the FLA community, the recent monthly Uncertainty Challenges and my buddies in Team Soaring in particular, have been instrumental in providing the accountability I needed to push myself through the fears and discomfort to get this workbook (and prior to that, my podcast) out into the world. For more info, see www.zenhabits.net.

ARTICLES AND ACADEMIC WORKS CONSULTED

Aonso-Diego, G., Secades-Villa, R., & González-Roz, A. (2023). Episodic future thinking for the prevention and treatment of health risk behaviors. *Papeles del Psicólogo, 44*(1), 8-14. https://doi.org/10.23923/pap.psicol.3005

Beck, J. S. (2020). *Cognitive behavior therapy* (3rd ed.). Guilford Press.

Brach, T. (2014) 'I Realized I Don't Have to Believe My Thoughts': Training in becoming mindful Retrieved from https://www.psychologytoday.com/intl/blog/finding-true-refuge/201403/i-realized-i-don-t-have-believe-my-thoughts

Clond, M., (2016) Emotional Freedom Techniques for Anxiety: A Systematic Review With Meta-analysis. *The Journal of Nervous and Mental Disease 204*(5):p 388-395, May 2016. | DOI: 10.1097/NMD.0000000000000483

Daniel T.O., Stanton C.M., & Epstein L.H. (2013) The future is now: reducing impulsivity and energy intake using episodic future thinking. *Psychol Sci. 2013 Nov 1;24*(11):2339-42. doi: 10.1177/0956797613488780. Epub 2013 Sep 10. PMID: 24022653; PMCID: PMC4049444.

Hölzel B., Carmody J., Vangel M., Congleton C., Yerramsetti S., Gard T., Lazar S. Mindfulness practice leads to increases in regional brain gray matter density. *Psychiatry Res.* 2011 Jan 30;191(1):36-43. doi: 10.1016/j.pscychresns.2010.08.006. Epub 2010 Nov 10. PMID: 21071182; PMCID: PMC3004979. https://www.ncbi.nlm.nih.gov/pmc/articles/PMC3004979/

Kovács, A.M. & Mehler, J. (2009) Cognitive gains in 7-month-old bilingual infants, Harvard University, Cambridge, MA, April 21, 2009, 106 (16) 6556-6560 https://doi.org/10.1073/pnas.0811323106

Lally, P., van Jaarsveld, C. H. M., Potts, H. W. W., & Wardle, J. (2010). How are habits formed: Modelling habit formation in the real world. *European Journal of Social Psychology, 40*(6), 998–1009. https://doi.org/10.1002/ejsp.674

Lardone, A., Liparoti, M., Sorrentino, P., Rucco, R., Jacini, F., Polverino, A., Minino, R., Pesoli, M., Baselice, F., Sorriso, A., Ferraioli, G., Sorrentino, G., & Mandolesi, L. (2018). Mindfulness Meditation Is Related to Long-Lasting Changes in Hippocampal Functional Topology during Resting State: A Magnetoencephalography Study. *Neural plasticity, 2018*, 5340717. https://doi.org/10.1155/2018/5340717

Liu, H., & Wu, L. (2021). Lifelong Bilingualism Functions as an Alternative Intervention for Cognitive Reserve Against Alzheimer's Disease. *Frontiers in psychiatry, 12*, 696015. https://doi.org/10.3389/fpsyt.2021.696015

Mishra, K.K. (2012) Optimism as Predictor of Good Life. (Unpublished research). https://www.researchgate.net/publication/239730158_Optimism_as_Predictor_of_Good_Life

Mooji (2020) "Bring your mind inside your heart and your world will not trouble you." YouTube, uploaded by Moojiji, 13 Sept 2020, www.youtube.com/watch?v=KAmXfBEEuE8

Moore, K. (2019) What Is Negativity Bias and How Can It Be Overcome? Retrieved from https://positivepsychology.com/3-steps-negativity-bias/

Nelms, J. & Bruce, L. (2016) A Systematic Review and Meta-Analysis of Randomized and Nonrandomized Trials of Clinical Emotional Freedom Techniques (EFT) for the Treatment of Depression. *EXPLORE: The Journal of Science and Healing*. 12. 10.1016/j.explore.2016.08.001.

Nelson, C. A. (2014). *Romania's Abandoned Children: Deprivation, Brain Development, and the Struggle for Recovery*. Harvard University Press.

Rand, K., Shanahan, M., Fischer, I., & Fortney, S. (2020). Hope and optimism as predictors of academic performance and subjective well-being in college students. *Learning and Individual Differences, 81*, 101906. https://doi.org/10.1016/j.lindif.2020.101906

Riopel, L. (2019). Mindfulness and the Brain: What Does Neuroscience Say? Retrieved from www.positivepsychology.com/mindfulness-brain-research-neuroscience/

Rothstein, L. & Stromme, D. (n.d.) "The RAS (Reticular Activating System," *Two For You*, short video lesson, University of Minnesota Extension. https://extension.umn.edu/two-you-video-series/ras

Sansone, R., & Sansone, L. (2010). Gratitude and well being: the benefits of appreciation. *Psychiatry (Edgmont (Pa. : Township)), 7*(11), 18–22.

Snow, M. A., & Brinton, D. M. (Eds.). (2017). *The content-based classroom: New perspectives on integrating language and content (2nd ed.).* Ann Arbor, MI: University of Michigan Press.

Stapleton, P., Baumann, O., O'Keefe, T., & Bhuta, S. (2022). Neural Changes after Emotional Freedom Techniques Treatment for Chronic Pain Sufferers. *Complementary Therapies in Clinical Practice, 49,* https://doi.org/10.1016/j.ctcp.2022.101653

Szalavitz, M. (2012) Q&A: Jon Kabat-Zinn Talks About Bringing Mindfulness Meditation to Medicine. Interview with Maia Szalavitz, healthland.time.com. January 11, 2012.

Tyng, C. M., Amin, H. U., Saad, M. N. M., & Malik, A. S. (2017). The Influences of Emotion on Learning and Memory. *Frontiers in psychology, 8,* 1454. https://doi.org/10.3389/fpsyg.2017.01454

RESOURCES FOR YOUR SPANISH

"Action is the foundational key to all success."
"La acción es la clave fundamental de todo éxito."
~ Pablo Picasso

· *Resources for your Spanish* ·

This section could be a whole book in itself, but I've tried to limit it so that it doesn't become too overwhelming. I've included passionate experts on a range of subjects. Please don't think you have to consume all the content; just dip in and choose the things that appeal to you the most and spark your curiosity and Spanish joy.

INSTAGRAM

Truth be told, I have a love-hate relationship with Instagram. I love that it's so visual, fun, informative, and appealing—for language learners and teachers alike (actually, for learning on any topic you can think of)—but I hate how it sucks me in and I can lose whole swathes of time, never to get it back.

That said, when used mindfully, Instagram is perfect for people who are short on time, as you can find many one- to two-minute videos that deliver great info very visually. Check out lots of accounts until you find a few favourites for boosting your Spanish. Just make sure you keep a joyful vocab notebook nearby to introduce the element of intention and curiosity, and to ensure you don't just end up mindlessly scrolling.

Here are a few suggestions for you to try. As always, follow the ones that most resonate with you and appeal to your learning style.

@heartfulspanishpodcast (joyful language immersion, Spanish fluency tips, positive psychology)
No es por echarme flores [literally "Not to flower throws at myself", i.e., not very modest of me], but let's start with my own little labour of love, my Heartful Spanish Podcast Instagram account.
My aim with my bilingual Instagram account is for Spanish learners who love the things I love—nature, positive psychology, spirituality, personal growth, and inspirational quotes—to soak up the language as they consume my (hopefully) uplifting and motivational posts. Check it out and see if it appeals to you.

@español_con_guada (Spanish language tips, fun chat)

Guada is a Spanish teacher from Spain, based in Italy. She has a fun, chatty approach. Guada's short videos are based on a variety of subjects related to Spain and the Spanish language, travel, living abroad, and pop culture.

@hablaconellas_ (Spanish language tips, fun dialogues, slang)

Desiré and Marisa are two Spanish teachers from Spain. They create funny and interesting dialogues, using real Spanish, often including lots of fun slang words that you won't find in the textbooks.

@spanish.with.vicky (Spanish language tips, fun dialogues, slang)

Vicky is a Spanish teacher from northern Spain. Her videos are funny and quirky, and she includes lots of play on words, common mistakes, and fun observations about the Spanish language. At the time of publication (August 2023), Vicky's account appears to have disappeared from Instagram, but she had a huge following so maybe she'll be back up and running again soon. If you're on TikTok, you can find her on there. (With the same name @spanish.with.vicky)

@spanishwithelisabeth (Spanish vocab, pronunciation, common mistakes, Argentina)

Elisabeth is a bilingual Spanish teacher who speaks American English and Argentine Spanish. She teaches snippets of Spanish vocab, pronunciation, and common mistakes.

@occimorons (cartoons, psychology, mental health, Spain)

Not a Spanish teacher, but just a lovely account for those who are interested in mental health and psychology. Pablo R Cocas the Spanish psychologist, author, and illustrator behind Occimorons—simple cartoon drawings, clear language, and beautiful and important messages about life, being human, and mental health.

@karencastilla.i (cartoons, positive psychology, emotional intelligence, Latin America)

Karen Castilla is a Latin American comic artist who creates adorable drawings on subjects related to positive psychology, growth mindset, gratitude, and emotional intelligence. Feel-good drawings and simple, insightful, and uplifting messages in Spanish.

@dra.josefagonzalez (short talks on holistic medicine, Chile)

Dr Josefa González is a qualified medical doctor from Chile who turned to holistic medicine in order to heal her own stress and mental health patterns. She discusses everything related to holistic health and integrative medicine: mindfulness, self-healing, emotional management, stress management, and spirituality.

Dra Josefa mostly gives short informational talks, which are a great learning aid for intermediate-advanced Spanish speakers who are interested in these subjects because she includes subtitles and on-screen captions.

@nai_jainai (kundalini yoga, awakening, Spain)

Fellow kundalini yoga lovers will love the work of wonderful teacher Naiara Santacoloma on Instagram.

Here's how Naiara describes herself:

"Profesora de kundalini yoga, entrenadora energética y/o investigadora del Ser. Comparto herramientas que nos ayudan a recordar lo que somos."

[Kundalini yoga teacher, energy trainer and/or researcher of Being. I share tools that help us remember who we are.]

What's not to love?

@jardineriafacil (gardening tips)

Budding gardeners and plant lovers will enjoy this Instagram account that shares simple, beautifully presented gardening tips for beginners and beyond.

LEARN SPANISH ON YOUTUBE

Español Con Guada

Guada, the lovely Spanish teacher I mentioned in the Instagram section, is also on YouTube, where she talks in more depth about similar subjects to those on her IG channel (Spanish language, travel, popular culture, etc.). Here's her Youtube channel:
www.youtube.com/@EspanolconGuada

Lightspeed Spanish

Gordon (a Brit) and Cynthia (from Spain) at Lightspeed Spanish have hundreds of fun and interesting videos on a variety of subjects for all levels of Spanish learners. Check them out here:
www.youtube.com/watch?v=PrXEAzantSk

Linguistix

Foreign language pronunciation expert Ruben, the founder of Linguistix, has a whole playlist on YouTube of short videos that will help you improve your Spanish accent in surprisingly different and creative ways.
www.youtube.com/@Linguistix
See also the Linguistix website: www.linguistixpro.com/spanish

· *Resources for your Spanish* ·

OTHER YOUTUBE CHANNELS IN SPANISH

BBVA Aprendemos Juntos 2030 (education, environment, sustainability, psychology, Spain)
www.youtube.com/@AprendemosJuntos

This is one of my favourite YouTube channels in Spanish. BBVA is a Spanish multinational financial services company, and this project, *Aprendemos Juntos* [We Learn Together], is dedicated to *la educación sostenible* [sustainable education] and creating a better world.

The YouTube channel has 3.6 million subscribers at the time of writing and hundreds of fantastic videos, mostly interviews with experts on a broad range of subjects related to science, education, and generally saving the planet. Uplifting, inspiring, and enlightening. The programmes can also be viewed on the BBVA Aprendemos Juntos 2030 website: www.aprendemosjuntos.bbva.com

El hormiguero (pop culture, various, Spain)
www.youtube.com/@elhormiguerooficial

El hormiguero is a popular TV program here in Spain, presented by the immensely likeable Pablo Motos. It's a light-hearted show that covers a wide variety of interests: pop culture, films, science, and trivia.

My favourite bit is when Pablo Motos interviews top Hollywood actors when they are in Spain promoting their latest films. It's fun to watch because you get to see them either speaking Spanish (always cool!) or, if not, attempting to cope with the terrifyingly stressful situation of being interviewed via a translator in their earpiece live on national telly.

La Sexta (national TV channel, Spain)
www.youtube.com/@laSexta

La Sexta is one of Spain's national terrestrial TV channels. Their YouTube site produces short and medium-length clips of a broad variety of TV programmes including La Sexta's longest-running show, "*El intermedio*" [the break/intermission] with El Gran Wyoming (real name: José Miguel Monzón Navarro, from Madrid). With his characteristic daft, irreverent humour, Wyoming talks about news and current affairs, generally poking fun at politicians and anyone currently in the public eye.

Have a browse through the myriad channels within La Sexta's broad range of programmes. There really is something for everyone. *Para gustos los colores* [literally: "for tastes, colours", i.e., everyone has different tastes], so I recommend you check out the channel to find the shows that appeal to you. I'll leave you with two other enormously popular programmes that might be of interest.

"*Lo de Évole*" is a show where Jordi Évole (one of my favourite TV presenters here in Spain) interviews interesting people from all walks of life—politicians, world leaders, prison inmates, ordinary heroes, and experts on all sorts of subjects. I love Évole because he is brilliant and *simpático* [friendly/ likeable], and he's not afraid to ask the hard-hitting questions.

"*Pesadilla en la cocina*" [Nightmare in the Kitchen] with Alberto Chicote is Spain's answer to Gordon Ramsay's "Kitchen Nightmares"—a reality television show revealing the goings-on behind the scenes in struggling restaurants. Just like his British counterpart, the host "El Chicote", as he is known affectionately, is not afraid to call a spade a spade. *No tiene pelos en la lengua.* [Literally: "He has no hairs on his tongue", i.e., he says it like it is.] Love him or hate him; you decide.

RTVE (national TV corporation, Spain)
www.youtube.com/@rtve/channels

RTVE (Radio Televisión Española) is Spain's national TV and radio corporation. I won't go down the rabbit hole of trying to summarise all the shows, but if you look at the channels tab on their YouTube site, you'll see programmes on a huge variety of different themes.

I will just share one interesting programme for those who have a love of travel: *Españoles en el mundo* [Spaniards in the World]. Each episode follows the life of a Spanish expat who lives in a different part of the world: Greenland, Kenya, Madagascar, Mumbai, Nepal—you name it. It's a fun way to discover faraway corners of this incredible world through the eyes of Spaniards who have upped sticks and made their home there.

Cocina con Addy [Cook with Addy] (cooking, Mexico)
www.youtube.com/@CocinadeAddy
If you're passionate about cooking and like watching videos to learn new recipes, you might enjoy this popular YouTube channel by passionate Yucatecan cook Addy. In her words, it's all about making "c*omida más sana sin sacrificar el sabor*" [healthier food without sacrificing the taste]. Addy specialises in vegetarian and vegan dishes, and her love of good food and nutrition shines through.

Dr Josefa González (holistic medicine, self-healing, Chile)
www.youtube.com/@dra.josefagonzalez
Dr Josefa, the Chilean doctor I mentioned in the Instagram section above, also has longer videos on YouTube where she offers classes, podcasts, and other resources, going into greater detail on the subjects of holistic medicine, mental and emotional health, and related topics.

Annel Vare (watercolour painting techniques)
www.youtube.com/annelvare
Annel Vare is a Spanish-speaking artist specialising in watercolours. You can find her videos on YouTube, Instagram, and Pinterest, where she teaches watercolour techniques and shares her beautiful artwork.

· *Heartful Spanish* ·

Jesús Calleja (nature lover, adventurer, Spain)
www.youtube.com/@jesuscalleja3487

Although he doesn't post a lot on YouTube, this Joyful resources for your Spanish section would not be complete if I didn't share one of Spain's national treasures with you. Jesús Calleja is a TV presenter, explorer, adventurer, climber, world traveller, lover of life, and an incorrigible joy spreader. On the website of *Cuatro*, the TV channel he works for, Calleja says he struggles to differentiate between work and holidays, "*porque como me lo paso tan bien currando*" [because I have such a good time when I'm working; *currar* is slang in Spain for the verb "to work"].

In his programmes, Jesús appears in the wildest corners of the world, sharing his love of this amazing planet, showing off his endurance and survival skills, spreading joy, and generally having a laugh with all the people he connects heart-to-heart with. You can't help but adore him.

In *Desafío extremo* [Extreme Challenge], Calleja shares his love of mountains and extreme adventures. He scales the world's highest mountains, scuba dives with sharks, crosses deserts, and chases tornadoes, amongst other wild escapades.

In *Planeta Calleja*, a kind of chat show meets travel and nature documentary, each episode sees Jesús take a different guest—mostly famous Spaniards—off on an adventure to some far-off place around the world. One of my favourite episodes was when he went to the Arctic Circle with Spanish journalist and TV presenter Mercedes Milá (the long-running presenter of *Gran hermano* [Big Brother], here in Spain). Here's a short clip I found on the internet. Such a delight. I challenge you to watch it without a smile on your face.

https://www.elperiodico.com/es/opinion/20170619/merceditas-en-bolas-en-el-artico-6115506

It's hard to say which is the best way for you to follow Jesús Calleja, because I did a little research, and he clearly spends more time living life than posting about it on social media (a lesson for us all). But he does have a page on Facebook, and he shares short snippets of his programmes on Instagram and YouTube occasionally too. You can find the full versions on the TV channel, *Cuatro*. Website link here: www.cuatro.com/

Wild Frank (Frank Cuesta, wildlife conservation, animal lover)

Another passionate, heart-led Spaniard, although possibly more of a Marmite type (i.e., you love him or you hate him) due to his abrupt, outspoken, and unpolished ways, Frank Cuesta is an animal lover, famous for presenting the enormously popular Spanish TV programmes "*Wild Frank*" and "*Frank de la jungla*" [Frank of the Jungle], where he would go into the jungles and the wildest corners of the planet to educate people about exotic animals and conservation projects.

In 2014, Frank gave up his hugely successful career in television to become a YouTuber. What famous TV presenter does that? A middle finger to success as determined by the rest of society.

Frank describes his YouTube channel like this: "*Canal dedicado al entendimiento y sobre todo al amor por la vida y la naturaleza*" [A channel dedicated to the understanding and especially to the love of life and nature]. There are a ton of videos you can watch that are guaranteed to boost your fluency in Spanish slang, ¡sí o sí! [literally: "yes or yes", meaning "for sure" or "without a doubt"].

Frank has a whole playlist of videos called "*Vídeos para sonreír*" [videos to (make you) smile]. Check out his channel here: www.youtube.com/@santuariolibertad

SPANISH RADIO

My recommendations in this section are very much Spain-based because they're what I know from living here. But if you love a particular Spanish-speaking country and would like to immerse yourself in its culture and language, it's well worth doing an internet search for the best radio stations there on subjects that interest you. (In fact, I'm going to do that right now, and rekindle my love of Mexican *rancheras,* a throwback to my unforgettable year in Mexico as a twenty-year-old undergrad.)

Cadena SER (news, sport, debates, entertainment, culture)
Cadena Ser is Spain's oldest radio station. Browse their website for subjects of interest to you, and you can listen right there. Some of their most popular programs include *A vivir que son dos días* [Get living, because it's just two days; an expression meaning "life's too short"], *La ventana* [The Window], and *Hoy por hoy* [Today for Today; an expression meaning "right now" or "at present"]. www.cadenaser.com

Onda Cero (pop music, news, and chat)
Onda Cero is another very popular national radio station here in Spain. One of its most loved programmes is *La rosa de los vientos* [The Rose of the Winds], on a variety of subjects related to science, technology, culture, humour, and history. *La brújula* [The Compass] is another well-liked show to look out for, sharing news, sports updates, and debates on politics and the economy. www.ondacero.es

Kiss FM (80's, 90's, current pop and chart music)
If you like pop and chart music, you might enjoy listening to Kiss FM, for "*lo mejor de los 80 y 90 hasta hoy*" [the best of the 80s and 90s up to today]. www.kissfm.es

· *Resources for your Spanish* ·

PODCASTS FOR SPANISH LEARNERS

Everyone will have different preferences in terms of topic and Spanish level (and therefore the degree of immersion), but here are a few language learners' podcasts you could check out to improve your Spanish listening.

The Heartful Spanish Podcast

¡Ya lo sé, ya lo sé; no tengo abuela! [literally, "I know it, I know it. I don't have a grandmother!" meaning, "I know, I know, it's terribly immodest of me!"], but I will start with my own personal joy project, The Heartful Spanish Podcast.

I've created this podcast as a stepping stone to help Spanish learners gain confidence in their listening skills prior to or alongside listening to native speakers. It focuses on the themes of personal growth, happiness, positive psychology, and living our best lives, and I believe that if you're passionate about these subjects like I am, you'll be more motivated to tune in and engage, and you'll soak up the new vocab effortlessly as you listen along.

The Heartful Spanish Podcast is available on Apple Podcasts, Spotify, Google Podcasts, and other major platforms, and all episodes are recorded in three versions: Spanish only, English only, and a bilingual version (which alternates a sentence of each). I've created it this way because everyone learns differently—some listeners prefer to listen in English first, to understand what's going on before attempting to tackle the Spanish, whereas others (even some complete beginners) are happy to dive straight into the Spanish version and treat it like a game, seeing which words they can understand. Yet others like the hand-holding of the bilingual version. How do *you* learn best?

Transcripts are available from my website www.heartfulspanish.com

"Notes In Spanish" and "Notes In Spanish Conversations"

Both of these podcasts are by Madrid-based bilingual couple Ben and Marina, friends of a friend of mine, who were two of the first creators of podcasts for Spanish learners. They have podcasts for all levels on a wide range of subjects, from travel and life in Spain to other subjects close to my heart like happiness, personal growth, and yoga.

In the lower levels (and on their YouTube channel), Ben and Marina talk a mixture of Spanish and English, whereas in the intermediate to advanced levels (and especially in Conversations), they speak only Spanish, so it's great for immersion.

www.notesinspanish.com

Fluent Spanish Express

The Fluent Spanish Express podcast is by Diego, a Spanish teacher from Spain, and it's especially good for intermediate and advanced level immersion as it's 100% in Spanish (no English translation or explanations). This podcast is great because it's very colloquial—Diego speaks how Spanish people really speak and doesn't simplify his language at all. He mostly chats about the Spanish language, interesting expressions, false friends, and common mistakes that he sees his students make. www.fluentspanish.express

Spanish and Go

This is another podcast by a bilingual couple, Jim (from the USA) and his wife May (from Mexico). In Spanish and Go, Jim and May talk about all sorts of subjects, mostly related to travel, as well as all things Latin American, but they throw in a few other interesting subjects too, such as language learning, improving your Spanish, and motivational tips. www.spanishandgo.com

PODCASTS IN SPANISH ON OTHER SUBJECTS

Todo Concostrina (history, Spain)

www.cadenaser.com/podcast/cadena-ser/cualquier-tiempo-pasado-fue-anterior/611/

Nieves Concostrina is a journalist and writer from Madrid with razor sharp wit and a cynical outlook. Her podcast, *Todo Concostrina*, describes all sorts of random anecdotes from the annals of history. It's a fun listen, and you'll pick up a ton of vocab. Real Spanish at its best. (Not for beginners!)

Nadie sabe nada (humour, Spain)

www.cadenaser.com/cadena-ser/nadie-sabe-nada/

In this fun podcast, two Spanish comedians chit-chat spontaneously on just about anything and everything you could possibly think of (and then some!). A great one for getting up to speed on Spanish slang.

The intro on the podcast's home page says it best:

Andreu Buenafuente y Berto Romero se sientan frente a frente, micro a micro, e improvisan. ¿Qué puede salir mal? El humor de estos dos genios es oro para tus orejas.

My translation: Andreu Buenafuente and Berto Romero sit face to face [literally: "forehead to forehead"], mic to mic, and improvise. What could go wrong? The humour of these two geniuses is gold for your ears.

TED en español (science, technology, creativity, business)

This podcast is a compilation of the best TED talks in Spanish. "*En el podcast de TED en español te invitamos a [...] escuchar ideas provocadoras y a desarrollar nuevas maneras de pensar.*" [In the *TED en español* podcast we invite you to [...] listen to thought-provoking ideas and develop new ways of thinking.] Hundreds of talks by passionate experts to awaken your curiosity on a wide range of subjects.

The TED website is a great resource for video versions of the talks. Go to www.ted.com/talks and select *español* from the drop down menu, and geek out to your heart's content.

The Wild Project, Jordi Wild (interviews pop culture, various, Spain)
www.youtube.com/c/TheWildProject

Jordi Wild's podcast is one of the most popular Spanish podcasts out there. Jordi has very free-flowing unscripted chats with Spanish guests that can often last for three or four hours or more. If you have time for that, it'll be great practice for your immersion in real Spanish.

In all honesty, this show is not my cup of tea, for the most part. I prefer shorter, to-the-point podcasts that pack a punch. I have, however, enjoyed some of Jordi's shorter YouTube clips on subjects that interest me (e.g., the recent ones about ChatGPT).

In Wild's words, here's what his podcast is about: "*Actualidad, deportes, charlas con los invitados más interesantes, ciencia, anécdotas y curiosidades, debates, filosofía, psicología, misterio, terror… y muchísimo más. Cada semana hablando claro y sin miedo sobre el mundo que nos rodea. ¡No te lo pierdas!*" [Current affairs, sports, chats with the most interesting guests, science, anecdotes and curiosities, debates, philosophy, psychology, mystery, horror, and so much more. Each week, speaking clearly and without fear about the world around us. Don't miss it!]

Give it a listen and see for yourself if it's for you.

Como hacer que te pasen cosas buenas (psychology, self-help, Spain)
www.marianrojas.com/podcast

Dr Marian Rojas Estapé is a Spanish psychiatrist and author. In her podcast, *Como hacer que te pasen cosas buenas* [how to make good things happen to you], she talks about interpersonal relationships, emotional intelligence, happiness, love, attachment, your inner voice, etc. All the things I love.

Entiende tu mente (psychology, Spain)
www.entiendetumente.info

Entiende tu mente (understand your mind) is a podcast all about psychology. Its slogan is "*20 minutos para entenderte mejor*" (20 minutes to understand yourself better), and the episodes are based on questions from ordinary people from Spain and Latin America answered by psychologists, on the full range of emotions and psychological issues, as well as book recommendations, the study of academic psychology, and more.

Durmiendo (sleep, wellbeing, positivity, Mexico)
www.podcastdurmiendo.com

The delightful *Durmiendo* is a short podcast to listen to at bedtime. It is designed to help you relax, reflect on your day, and get into a positive mindset for a good night's sleep. Each episode lasts for less than 10 minutes, and the warm, gentle voice of the male Mexican presenter is perfect for sending you off to dreamland with your ear attuned to *español* and self-love. Beautifully affirming.

The sister podcast *Despertando*, by the same producers, is equally delightful. Short episodes on living your best life, spirituality, and positive psychology.

OTHER USEFUL WEBSITES FOR YOUR SPANISH

La Real Academia Española (RAE)

www.rae.es

La Real Academia Española [The Spanish Royal Academy] is a 300-year-old national organisation comprised of a panel of 46 Spanish language experts (illustrious writers, poets, academics, etc.) who are responsible for maintaining the cohesion of the Spanish language in the Spanish-speaking world in the face of the constant evolution of the language.

It's a unique concept, really, and something we don't have in the English-speaking world. And this is going to be a controversial opinion, but despite the efforts of these illustrious experts over the last 300+ years, I'm not sure there actually *is* a whole lot more cohesion in the Spanish language around the world than there is in the English language in Anglophone countries.

I can, however, see a huge benefit of the RAE in one area: homogenising the rules for academic writing and publishing. In the English-speaking world, there are different systems of punctuation and different style guides, depending on whether you're following the Oxford, Harvard, APA, or whatever system. This can be a nightmare for freelancers or anyone who works with a variety of publishers, like I do as a translator. (It plays havoc with your punctuation!) In that sense, I can definitely see the advantage of having one set of guidelines for all.

The RAE publishes its own Spanish dictionary, el *Diccionario de la Real Academia Española*, which is *the* dictionary par excellence of the Spanish language and arguably the best place for advanced-level or native Spanish speakers to look up a word to gain clarity on its meaning. You can find the online version of the dictionary of the RAE here: www.dle.rae.es

Instituto Cervantes (Spanish language and Hispanic cultures)

www.cervantes.es

The Instituto Cervantes is another national institution here in Spain dedicated to the Spanish language and culture. Its focus is specifically aimed at the teaching of Spanish as a foreign language. The Instituto Cervantes' head office is in Madrid, but the *Instituto* has branches in 88 different cities in 45 countries across all five continents, where they teach Spanish as a foreign language, disseminate cultural knowledge, and create events for students and lovers of Hispanic cultures.

The Instituto Cervantes also organises language exams for official certification (recognised internationally) of the different Spanish language levels, which you can do in person in over 85 countries in the world and also online. The highest-level certificates are often required for foreigners seeking entrance to Spanish-speaking universities or access to some jobs in Spain.

The website of the Instituto Cervantes also has a useful forum for any (Spanish) language-related questions you may have.

Alba Learning (a free online library of books and audio books in Spanish)

www.albalearning.com

This fabulous website, curated by literature lover Alba, is home to the biggest collection of online text and audio versions of the classics of Spanish literature. Novels, short stories, poems—you name it—from all kinds of authors over the centuries from Spain and Latin America (as well as plenty of other literary classics from other languages translated into Spanish).

Literature lovers, bookmark this site and come back to Alba's treasure chest often, to get your fill of Spanish reading joy.

Heartful Spanish Facebook Group

www.facebook.com/groups/474872237041841

I set up this free Facebook group when I launched my Heartful Spanish podcast. It has been a little quiet around there lately, but it would be a great place to look for a language exchange partner (from among the native Spanish speakers in the group) or an accountability buddy (from the fellow Spanish learners) to help you keep up your joyful language practice habits.

Don't be shy! Post a short intro about who you are and what you're looking for. This could be a game changer in your journey to fluency.

My Little Spanish Notebook www.mylittlespanishnotebook.wordpress.com

This is my first labour of love, my blog, which I started just over 10 years ago. Mostly in English, I write all about the Spanish words that spark my curiosity and send me running for the dictionary. It's the internet version of my very own joyful vocabulary notebook, a collection of the words and phrases that light up my radar.

Word Reference www.wordreference.com

WordReference has a number of different forums where you can ask for people's opinions and advice on the usage of specific terms and phrases in Spanish (and other languages). Rather than actively posting myself, I mostly just stumble across these posts by Googling the meaning of certain terms in Spanish or English. It's very helpful to read the threads and glean different opinions from translators, native speakers, and other enthusiasts in different countries around the world on their understanding of the usage of different words and expressions.

Linguee www.linguee.es

I use Linguee in a similar way to WordReference: to look up different meanings, interpretations, and usage of words from various sources (in Spanish and other languages). It's not opinion-based, like WordReference, but more like a database of real snippets from online publications where the word or expression in question has been used in context. Super useful for getting the nuances that the dictionaries don't always capture.

Conversation exchange websites

Try these websites for finding conversation partners to practice your Spanish with:

- www.mylanguageexchange.com
- www.openlanguageexchange.com
- www.easylanguageexchange.com

Websites for Spanish lessons

Check out these websites and try a few Spanish teachers until you find one you love.

- Italki www.italki.com
- Preply www.preply.com
- Verbalplanet www.verbalplanet.com

ChatGPT

www.openai.com/chatgpt

Visit the Open AI website for more information on how to set up an account with ChatGPT. Once you've done that, you can use ChatGPT as your own personal Spanish conversation partner, available any time of day or night. Have fun experimenting with this new technology, and see if you find it fun and helpful for your Spanish.

APPS FOR YOUR SPANISH

AnkiApp (for memorising vocabulary)

Anki allows you to create flashcards to memorise new or tricky words. The app also has ready-made Spanish flashcards that you can choose from to expand your vocabulary.

Using flashcards can provide the extra focus you need to cement those words that just won't stick with other methods. I use them occasionally for unusual words I learn (from my life here in Spain or in my work as a translator).

HiNative

The HiNative app connects you with native speakers in different languages around the world. The free version allows you to ask questions about usage, whether something sounds natural, etc. The premium version is ad-free and includes additional features, such as the ability to post a certain number of posts per month, to ensure you get multiple answers from different viewpoints.

Language exchange apps (for conversation practice)

Check out these popular conversation exchange apps for practising with native speakers.

- HelloTalk
- Tandem
- Speaky

BOOKS

Here is a brief selection of books by Spanish and Latin American authors you could dip into, from comics and simplified reading books for Spanish learners to more advanced-level novels and classics of Spanish and Latin American literature.

It's hard to narrow down book recommendations in just a few pages and try to include all levels of Spanish learner, but here I've selected a mixture of books that have touched my mind and/or heart, and ones I think might touch yours.

Remember, it's OK—in fact, it's ideal—if the books you read are slightly above your level of comprehension, as this will mean you get used to getting the gist and pushing on through the discomfort of not understanding everything. This is fabulous practice for improving your Spanish fast, *but only if it feels like fun for you*. The moment it starts to feel too much like a chore, lighten the load by setting smaller daily goals, or switch to something more appealing and enjoyable for you.

BEGINNER TO INTERMEDIATE LEVEL

Comics

10 años con mafalda by quino (Argentina)

This is a compilation of the much-loved Argentine comic *Mafalda*. Written in the 1960s and 70s, *Mafalda* is a satire on the absurdities of the adult world seen through the eyes of an outspoken, wise-beyond-her-years six-year-old girl who cares deeply about the state of humanity. A series of smaller books published by Distribooks is also available (*Mafalda* 1–10).

Gracias by 72Kilos (Spain)

72 Kilos (real name: Óscar Alonso) is a Spanish comic artist from Bilbao, in the Basque Country. His creations are delightful, witty reflections on what it is to be human, and the language is mostly very simple. *Gracias* is uplifting and thought-provoking. Other titles by the same author include *El mundo es un regalo* and *Las vidas que dibujamos*.

Esas cosas que nos pesan by Pablo R. Coca (Spain)

Illustrator and writer Pablo R. Coca, also known as @occimoron on Instagram, calls himself "*el psicólogo que va al psicólogo*" [the psychologist who goes to the psychologist]. This is his first book, which deals with the subject of mental health and anxiety in a compassionate, upbeat way. Simple language and endearing illustrations describe the reality of the process for anyone who ends up choosing to go to therapy.

Short stories
Short Stories in Spanish by Olly Richards

Olly Richards has a vast collection of books for learners of Spanish and other languages, including a number of short story books in simplified Spanish for beginners and intermediate levels, with vocabulary sections and English translations and explanations.

As well as his short story books, Richards offers simplified reading books on a wide range of subjects such as climate change, history (the First and Second World Wars, revolutions), the human body, and western philosophy. Choose a subject you're naturally interested in or you want to learn more about, and you'll deepen your understanding of that subject as you improve your language skills without even realising. Two birds, one stone and all that!

Children's books

The *Manolito Gafotas* series by Elvira Lindo (Spain)

The *Manolito Gafotas* books by Elvira Lindo are a series of humorous stories aimed at children but enjoyed by adults too. The protagonist, Manolito, is a chatty little boy with big glasses (hence the nickname "*Gafotas*") who tells amusing anecdotes about his life with his little brother *el Imbécil* [the Idiot] and other family members in the Madrid *barrio* [neighbourhood] of Carabanchel.

ADVANCED LEVEL

Short Stories

If you're keen to read more in Spanish but you prefer something a little more manageable in size before progressing to whole novels and other books, here are some advanced-level short stories to whet your appetite.

La increíble y triste historia de la cándida Eréndira y de su abuela desarmada y otros cuentos [The Incredible and Sad Tale of Innocent Eréndira and Her Heartless Grandmother] by Gabriel García Márquez

The main title in this anthology narrates the mishaps and misadventures of fourteen-year-old Eréndira, who is cruelly mistreated by her authoritarian grandmother but never gives up her dream of running away and finding freedom. The rest of the stories are much shorter and include the quintessential García Márquez story *Muerte constante más allá del amor* [Death Constant Beyond Love], parts of which were incorporated into the film version of *Eréndira* by Ruy Guerra.

Historias de Cronopios y de Famas by Julio Cortázar

This compilation of intriguing short stories is full of metaphor and fantasy. Big-hearted, emotion-led *Cronopios* and efficient-minded, logical *Famas* are invented beings in a world of symbolism and surrealism. Which of the two do you relate to the most?

Déjame que te cuente [Let me tell you (a story)] and *Cuentos para pensar* [Stories to make you think] by Jorge Bucay

Argentine psychologist and author Jorge Bucay creates simple stories (often new versions of classic tales and legends) to offer symbolic lessons on life and humanity to his patients and anyone who loves a bit of psychological reflection.

Plays

If you enjoy theatre, whether going to see a play or reading a script, here are a few classics from the first half of the twentieth century that might elevate your Spanish joy levels. Try reading the dialogues out loud for full joy-boosting effect.

Trilogía rural by Federico García Lorca (Spain)

(Bodas de sangre, Yerma, and *La casa de Bernarda Alba)*

This trilogy—three of Lorca's most famous plays—is set in *la España profunda* [rural, "backwater" Spain] of the early 20th century. Rich in symbolism and poetic language, Lorca's central themes include love, oppression, myth, nature, passion, and death.

I discovered Lorca in my teenage years, and although reading his plays was a challenge for me because I didn't understand half of the words, I loved them because I was deeply moved by the poetic imagery and symbolism.

Poetry

Reading poetry is another wonderful way to elevate your Spanish joy in small doses that can pack a punch. It's also great practice for enjoying the Spanish language for the pure love of it because reading poetry can often be more of an emotive, perceptive experience than a logical, cerebral one.

When reading poetry (in Spanish or in any language), I don't recommend you spend too much time pondering the meaning of individual words, unless, of course, you are fuelled by curiosity and delight to do so. Instead, just relish in the beauty of the words and notice the emotions and sensations they produce in you.

And if you're not yet confident enough to read solely in Spanish, there are many online sources of bilingual poetry in Spanish and English. See, for example, the websites of The Poetry Foundation at www.poetryfoundation.com, Poetry in Translation at www.poetryintranslation.com, and Alba Learning at www.albalearning.com.

Mario Benedetti (Uruguay)

"*No te salves*" by Benedetti is one of my favourite Latin American poems. Its language is fairly simple (for upper intermediate to advanced learners), and it is especially good for practising the negative imperative in Spanish (i.e., "*No hagas esto; no hagas aquello*," meaning, "Don't do this; don't do that").

Alfonsina Storni (Argentina)

An early voice in feminist poetry, Argentine poet Alfonsina Storni wrote in exquisite language that is, for the most part, simple to understand. Some of her most famous poems include "*Voy a dormir*" (I'm Going to Sleep), "*Tú me quieres blanca*" (You Want Me White), *Hombre pequeñito* (Little Man), and "*Han venido*" (They've Come).

Federico García Lorca (Spain)

Many of Lorca's most famous poems (e.g., *Romance de la luna luna* [Ballad of the Moon, Moon], *Romance sonámbulo* [Sleepwalking Ballad], and *La casada infiel* [The Unfaithful Wife]) can be found on the internet, including some translated into English on the websites of The Poetry Foundation or Poetry in Translation (see above for details).

Lorca's poems are, of course, widely available in Spanish, including on this website, dedicated exclusively to disseminating the works of the much-loved Andalusian poet: www.federicogarcialorca.net

Julio Cortázar (Argentina)

Every time it rains and I find myself stuck inside feeling wistful, I read or listen to the short poem *"Tristes gotas"* [Sad (Rain) Drops] by Julio Cortázar. It never fails to bring me back to the present moment and connect me with the childlike delight of watching raindrops form and glide down the windowpane.

Other poems you could try include *Para leer en forma interrogativa* [To Be Read in an Interrogative Manner], *Una carta de amor* [A Love Letter], and *Los amigos* [Friends], all of which are widely available on the internet. (See, for example, www.poeticous.com.)

Pablo Neruda (Chile)

Nobel poet Pablo Neruda wrote around 3,500 poems during his lifetime. *Veinte poemas de amor y una canción desesperada* [Twenty Love Poems and a Song of Despair] is one of his most popular collections of poetry.

For those less comfortable reading Spanish poetry, a simple online search for "Pablo Neruda poems bilingual" will produce a number of bilingual resources for you to peruse, some of which also have audio versions read by native Spanish speakers.

Poems in Spanish (with audio)

An especially good source for audio recordings of poems in Spanish (sometimes with their English translations) is the above-mentioned website Alba Learning at www.albalearning.com.

Novels

Patria [Homeland] by Fernando Aramburu (Spain)

An engaging saga, spanning a 30-year period and narrating the (fictional) story of two women whose friendship and families were profoundly affected by the terrorism in the Basque Country. This book did more for my understanding of what was going on in the Basque Country than a gazillion news reports.

La casa de los espíritus [The House of the Spirits] by Isabel Allende (Chile)
Reality and magic are interwoven in this much-loved saga about a landowning family in Chile. If you like romantic fiction and love the magical and mystical, this novel is a great introduction to the works of Isabel Allende.

La catedral del mar [The Cathedral of the Sea] by Ildefonso Falcones (Spain)
I enjoyed this epic tale of the (fictional) human stories behind the building of a cathedral in 13th-century Barcelona. The vivid descriptions of medieval life really fired up my imagination and changed my experience of visiting any ancient church or cathedral forever. The narrative is heavy-going in parts, but it's well worth persevering (if only for the sense of achievement after reading a 600+ page novel in Spanish!).

Como agua para chocolate [Like Water for Chocolate] by Laura Esquivel (Mexico)
Highly cinematic in its imagery, *Como Agua Para Chocolate* is an easy read and a firm favourite of romantic novel readers and Mexico lovers. Set during the time of the Mexican Revolution, this novel blends Mexican culture and traditions, recipes, stories of impossible love, and magical occurrences. A film version of the book was made by Mexican film director Alfonso Arau, the author's then-husband.

El coronel no tiene quien le escriba [No One Writes to the Colonel] by Gabriel García Márquez (Colombia)
This poignant novella tells the story of an aging colonel who lives on the brink of poverty in ever-hopeful expectation of receiving his government pension. Other books by García Márquez include the all-time Latin American classic *100 años de soledad* [One Hundred Years of Solitude], as well as many other novels.

La tregua [The Truce] by Mario Benedetti (Uruguay)
A brief novel about a lonely, widowed accountant who unexpectedly falls in love, which gives him a "truce" from his sad and meaningless existence. This one's an easy read but a bit of a tear-jerker.

Pedro Párramo by Juan Rulfo (Mexico)
This is a classic of Mexican literature and one of the precursors to magical realism. It's a lyrical story of shattered dreams, in which the borders between reality and hallucinations and between life and death are blurred. Set in rural Mexico in the 1920s, *Pedro Párramo* tells the story of Juan Preciado, who promised his mother on her deathbed that he would return to the (fictional) town of Comala to seek payback from his long-lost father, the eponymous Pedro Párramo.

Autobiography

Vivir para contarlo by Gabriel García Márquez
I enjoyed Gabo's autobiography, *Vivir para contarlo,* immensely. Fascinating insights into his childhood in Colombia and the beginnings of the magical realism that would later dominate the novels of this adored *maestro* of Latin American literature.

Paula by Isabel Allende
Isabel Allende's daughter, Paula, fell into a coma in 1991. Allende wrote this captivating autobiography from her daughter's bedside in hospital. *Paula* recounts the author's memories of her childhood, her family's past, the turbulent presidency of her uncle Salvador Allende and the 1973 coup d'état in Chile, as well as the family's subsequent exile, interspersed with present-moment reflections and observations on her daughter's heartbreaking situation. The whole story is infused with Allende's characteristic blurring of the borders between reality and fantasy.

TV SERIES IN SPANISH

I don't watch a lot of Spanish TV, so I haven't got too many must-see recommendations for you, but if you haven't already watched *Casa de papel* and *Relatos salvajes,* both of those are excellent and would be a great place to start.

Casa de papel [Literally, "House of Paper" but known as "Money Heist" in English] is a highly acclaimed Spanish bank robbery drama on Netflix.

Relatos salvajes [Wild/Savage Stories] is not actually a TV series but a hard-to-categorise Argentine film containing six separate short films, somewhere between a psychological thriller and a dark comedy, on a variety of themes about how humans behave when pushed to the limit. Brilliantly done. Available on Prime Video, Netflix, HBO Max, etc.

Other well-rated series that you could check out include the following:

Velvet, a historical drama set in a department store in the 1950s (Prime Video)

El tiempo entre costuras [Literally, "The time between the seams" but known as "The Time in Between" in English], the story of a young dressmaker in Madrid at the outbreak of the Civil War (Prime Video)

Gran hotel [Grand hotel], a crime romance series set in the 1900s in a fictional town on the coast of Catalonia (Prime Video)

El ministerio del tiempo [The Ministry of Time], a science fiction series in which the time-travelling protagonists ensure Spanish history proceeds as it should (Netflix)

Vis a vis [known as "Locked Up" in English], Spain's answer to "Orange is the New Black" (Prime Video)

La catedral del mar [The Cathedral of the Sea], the TV series based on the book I recommended by Ildefonso Falcones about the building of a medieval cathedral in Barcelona (Netflix)

CHROME EXTENSIONS FOR SUBTITLES

These two incredibly valuable Chrome extensions for language learners work on desktop and laptop computers running Windows and MacOS. Highly recommended for language learning by immersion.

Language Reactor (previously known as "Language Learning With Netflix")

Language Reactor allows you to watch your favourite programs on Netflix or YouTube with bilingual subtitles and precise playback controls for you to repeat anything you want to hear again. It also has a dictionary function for you to look up Spanish words that spark your curiosity.

Subtitles for Language Learning (Prime Video)

Similarly, the Subtitles for Language Learning Chrome extension allows you to watch Amazon Prime shows with subtitles, dictionary references, and grammar explanations. You can also slow down the viewing pace, which can help boost your confidence when starting out.

SPANISH AND LATIN AMERICAN CINEMA

It would be impossible to provide an exhaustive list of film recommendations to suit all tastes, so instead I'll just leave you with a few suggestions of highly rated films and successful directors and actors for you to keep an eye out for.

Look for these big names of *cine en español* wherever you usually watch movies: Netflix, HBO, Prime Video, etc. Enjoy!

Pedro Almodóvar (director, Spain)
Many of the films of fabulously outlandish film director Pedro Almodóvar are worth watching. Try *Todo sobre mi madre* (1999), *Volver* (2006), starring Penelope Cruz, or the Oscar-winning *Hable con ella* (1999).

Guillermo del Toro (director, Mexico)
Academy Award-winning director Guillermo del Toro has created some of his films in his native Spanish, including the dark fantasy *El laberinto del Fauno* ("Pan's Labyrinth", 2006) and the gothic horror film *El espinazo del diablo* ("The Devil's Backbone", 2001).

Ricardo Darín (actor, director, Argentina)
Ricardo Darin has starred in 40 or so films, including the above-mentioned *Relatos salvajes* (2014) and the superb *Argentina, 1984* (2022). Other noteworthy titles include *El secreto de sus ojos* [The Secret in Their Eyes] (2009) and *Nueve reinas* [Nine Queens] (2000).

Luis Tosar (actor, Spain)
Galician actor Luis Tosar tends to choose thought-provoking films on social and political themes. Tosar won awards for *Te doy mis ojos* [Take My Eyes] (2003), *Los lunes al sol* [Mondays in the Sun] (2004), and *Celda 211* [Cell 211] (2009). He also starred alongside Penelope Cruz in the recent *En los márgenes* [On the Fringe] (2022).

Gael García Bernal (actor, Mexico)
Mexican actor Gael García Bernal has played the lead in a variety of award-winning films. His works include the brilliant (but violent) *Amores perros* [Love's a Bitch] (2000), the popular biopic about the life of Che Guevara, *Diarios de motociclista* [The Motorcycle Diaries] (2004), and the Oscar-nominated road film *Y tu mamá también* [And Your Mother Too] (2001) by Alfonso Cuarón.

Lola Dueñas (actress, Spain)

Lola Dueñas, from Barcelona, has starred in a number of successful films, including Pedro Almodóvar's *Abrazos rotos* [Broken Embraces] (2009) and *Volver* [Returning] (2006), as well as Alejandro Amenábar's *Mar adentro* [The Sea Inside] (2004).

Carmen Maura (actress, Spain)

Madrid-born actress Carmen Maura has appeared in a number of Almodóvar films including *Mujeres al borde de un ataque de los nervios* [Women on the Verge of a Nervous Breakdown], (2000), and *Volver*, (2006), as well as the crime-thriller comedy *La comunidad* [The Community], (2000) directed by Álex De La Iglesia.

FilmIn Website (for streaming films, series, etc.) www.filmin.es

FilmIn is a Spain-based portal for streaming movies, shorts, series, and independent films on demand. If you're in Spain, you can opt for Premium or Premium+ membership, the latter including an additional three premier titles per month. For readers not based in Spain, the catalogue may still be of use to you for inspiration on what to watch, as it is a fantastic reference for info on the world's best films, series, festivals, award-winners, etc. from this century and last, each work summarised succinctly in Spanish and rated out of 10.

I particularly love the Filmin section *Colecciones* [Collections] on the website, which is like a database where you can peruse titles according to all kinds of wonderful categories, for example, *Parejas icónicas* [iconic couples/duos], *Grandes artistas que quizá no conoces* [great artists you may not know], *Top 100 LATAM* [top 100 Latin American films], *Las amas o las odias* [you love them or you hate them], *Grandes revelaciones del cine español* [great revelations of Spanish cinema], *Ha nacido una Estrella; La película con la que brillaron* [a star is born; the film that made them shine], and many more.

SHINE YOUR LIGHT

"When you share your unique light, bit by bit, you light up the lives of those around you. And, one by one, you inspire them to light up too. It's a chain reaction. And before long, the whole world lights up. Your light is contagious."

"Cuando compartes tu luz única, poco a poco, iluminas la vida de quienes te rodean. Y, uno a uno, los inspiras a iluminarse también. Es una reacción en cadena. Y en poco tiempo, todo el mundo se ilumina. Tu luz es contagiosa."

~ Rebecca Campbell

GO FORTH ON YOUR OWN UNIQUE JOURNEY

It's all about the joy, my friend! (But you've probably noticed that already if you've got to this point in the workbook.) Your Spanish practice must feel good to you, and it is time you started being kinder to yourself on your journey to fluency. You'll get there a lot quicker that way.

The seventh-century Persian poet Rumi said, "Let yourself be silently drawn by the strange pull of what you really love. It will never lead you astray." And, as in life, so in language learning.

Your heart knows the easy way to learn languages: through openness, curiosity, and wonder. So, follow its wisdom, do what lights you up on your self-led Spanish-learning journey, be present to your emotions, and you can't go wrong.

If you notice yourself having a hard time or beating up on yourself for your lack of progress, thank your emotional compass for that information. It's just letting you know that you're not on the fastest, easiest route to fluency and that you need to change track. Listen to your inner wisdom and course-correct accordingly.

Everyone learns differently, and *you* are the expert of you. You already have all the answers inside of you, and you are more than capable of learning Spanish to a high level of fluency. But don't aim to get there all at once; just set small, doable goals and create consistent habits, and before you know it, you'll be improving in leaps and bounds, well on your way to ease and flow in Spanish.

Now, take a couple of different-coloured highlighter pens or crayons and skim back through this workbook, underlining the *affirmations* (colour one) and *exercises* (colour two) that most appeal to you. Start with those and take it from there. Next, read through the "Resources for your Spanish" section and choose a few films, books, series, apps, Instagram accounts, websites, or whatever that look like they'd be a fun way for you to practise Spanish in mini-immersions.

Revisit your feel-good Spanish learning plan (see p.148), set yourself up with some accountability, and track your progress, making sure you build the habit of doing little bits of fun and joyful Spanish practice regularly throughout your week. Place reminders or symbols around your home where you'll see them to remind yourself that you're on the joyful, easeful path to fluency.

The world needs you to shine your own unique and beautiful light. The Spanish-speaking world needs to hear your voice. Are you ready to step up to the challenge? Of course you are, my lovely!

Enjoy the journey to fluency, beautiful soul. Your greatness awaits you.

NEXT STEPS

Visit my website at www.heartfulspanish.com and download one of the free Heartful Spanish habit trackers and the feel-good Spanish fluency plan to get you started with your own unique self-led journey to fluency.

LET'S CONNECT

I cannot wait to hear how this workbook has helped you reset the course of your Spanish learning and pick it up with positivity and confidence. Do share your experience with me via the Heartful Spanish Facebook group, on Instagram at @heartfulspanishpodcast, or drop me an email at louisa@heartfulspanish.com. I'd love to know what worked well for you and any bits that might need tweaking.

It's my mission to spread more language joy in the world and to show people that, through simple practices and mindset shifts like the ones I've presented in this workbook, fluency is available to everyone, it doesn't cost a lot, and it isn't hard work or boring—in fact, the fastest route is quite the opposite. You can do it, beautiful reader. I know it with all my heart.

SPREAD THE WORD

I hope you've found this workbook helpful. I'd be forever grateful if you'd take a moment to leave me a review on Amazon or on Goodreads. A sincere review from you will help this little book reach the people who need it. Even a short review makes a big difference. Thank you.

ACKNOWLEDGEMENTS

"At times, our own light goes out and is rekindled by a spark from another person. Each of us has cause to think with deep gratitude of those who have lighted the flame within us."

"A veces, nuestra propia luz se apaga y se reaviva con una chispa de otra persona. Cada uno de nosotros tiene motivos para pensar con profunda gratitud en aquellos que han encendido la llama dentro de nosotros."

~ Albert Schweitzer, philosopher, writer, Nobel Peace Prize winner

· Acknowledgements ·

A huge heartful thank you to my amazing beta readers, Sarah H, Sion D, Linda E, Kelly P, Trina O, and Krista P, who read through an earlier, messier version of this workbook and gave me lots of insightful and encouraging feedback. I really appreciate your time and generosity, ladies.

I couldn't have pushed through the fear and uncertainty of getting this passion project out in the world without a gazillion Focusmate partners and my online accountability buddies in the fabulous Project We (Soul Explorers), Fearless Living Academy (FLA), and IWBB (International Women in Business) communities, especially my fellow Team Soaring members from the FLA, my soul sisters at Project We, and my Vaultini *amigas* at IWBB.

I'm grateful to all of my friends and role models who inspire me to aim to be the best version of myself, especially those who've paved the way and led by example to show me it's not completely impossible to start a podcast, write a book, and put yourself out there on the "interwebs", or have modelled success and determination in a million other ways. Special mention to the wonderful Brigitte G, without whom I would no doubt still be tilting at windmills and pummelling my fists at the Audacity screen. Also to Ursula T, for being my partner in "tweaking" all these years and for the gazillion productivity hacks and (more recently) the game-changing coaching. And to Chus, my creativity buddy (María J. Cuesta), for sharing her knowledge of the writing world and shining her unique light so brightly. Also, heartfelt awe and gratitude to the talented Stacia S, who generously read through a very late draft of this manuscript and helped me make it "zing" a bit more.

Last but not least, I am deeply grateful to Alejandro for being my rock, my partner in adventures, and my (eternally patient—mostly!) proofreader of practically everything I've ever published in Spanish on the internet. *Te quiero*. Thanks, also, to our boys, not-so-mini proofreaders in the making. We love you.

Notes

Notes

Notes

Notes

Notes

Printed in Great Britain
by Amazon

30568182R00136